Perfectly Imperfect

Perfectly Imperfect

My Story of Abuse and Victimhood

Jenifer Krause

PremaMateria.com

CONTENTS

CONTENTS

CONTENTS

This book was written in order to help just one person, any one person, so that you know you are not alone. I dedicate it to all the past, present and future versions of you and I for we are all interconnected and when one of us feels pain, we all do on some sort of cosmic level. May this book and my life be an indication that we can overcome so much more than we give ourselves credit for, that we can find our inner truth and inner knowing to help guide us to healing ourselves and the world around us.

Thank you to all who have been a part of my life, the ones that have hurt me, I forgive you and I love you. The ones that have helped me, I love you and thank you just the same. My life and our relationships have been perfectly imperfect. Thank you for your time and patience. You know who you are and I am forever grateful.

Introduction

This story may surprise you, and if it doesn't then I will be the one to be surprised. You see, any time I have ever shared any of my life growing up with friends, therapists, marriage counselors, coworkers or colleagues, I have always gotten that "look". That look is one of pity, of concern, but mostly it's a look of, *I am so sorry that you went through that terrible thing*. Pity has no place in my kind of happy life, no place at all. The moment you start to feel sorry for yourself, you give up. That's it. You will start heading in a downward spiral, and it only goes faster the more you go down it. I know, because I have been there. I spent time there and I want to share with you how I was able to get out of it.

Our marriage counselor had actually made me really freaked out at how overly empathetic she was towards me after hearing a few of the stories I am about to share with you. Up until I was an adult I had only told a few therapists of what I went through while I was actually going through it. Back then, I wasn't taken seriously and so my life continued as if it were all a lie. I know however, that I am not the only one that has suffered in life. My life wasn't a lie, and as terrible as it was, it made me who I am today, and I can say that I am proud of who I have become. I no longer suffer, I am no longer silent and am now living. I have known for a long time that I would have to share my story. Sharing is not only a way for me to heal therapeutically from the trauma I have suffered, but had I known that there were other people like me out there in the world, I think I would have been able to heal faster and not have had to go through so much self hatred which was truly unnecessary. There is nothing worse than feeling alone. Feeling alone made me isolated. It made me shy, embarrassed, it made me nervous to talk or to make friends. It made me stutter whenever I had to say anything in front of a group of people. Feeling alone made me think I was worthless and a waste of a human being. Feeling alone made me turn to drugs and alcohol. Feeling alone made me want to die. If I had only known there was something else out there. And that I wasn't the only one who felt like this perhaps I would have been able to turn things around quicker and much easier.

I truly believe life happens the way that it is supposed to. Of course we all have free will. We can still choose differently than what our fate has in store for us. But as long as you pay attention, don't fall for the tricks of the mindless chatter going on in your own head, you will be able to overcome anything and you will be able to live to your full potential. We each have a path and I have finally found one that is worthy of me.

I wrote this in pieces, over many, many years. The first half about my childhood was written about 8 years ago when I was still learning to heal myself and had a lot of anger still left inside me that I wasn't as aware of compared to now. I am extremely grateful for everything I have gone through, and that voice I wrote from was a version of me that needed to speak up where she was and tell her side of her own story.

The same goes for the middle part of the book as well. Again, written some time ago, while I was actually going through my divorce. My mental and emotional states were extremely fragile. That still shouldn't take away from my experience and where I was at the time.

The rest of my story, in between these covers anyway, tells how I changed my life around and became connected, intuitively. How my transformation process happened and how difficult, yet rewarding my life has become. I wouldn't have changed it for anything.

On a legal note, all names and some events have been changed to prevent any sort of backlash as these things are extremely sensitive in nature. These things and stories or just that, MY stories and they are my own experiences and interpretations of my own truth. Not to be confused with anyone else's experiences or truths that I am connected with. We all have our own, and that doesn't take away from me having mine, or you having yours. All is valid.

1

This is Only the Beginning

Paralyzed

I am 5 Years old. My earliest memories. We lived in this trailer park in Bensalem, Pennsylvania, in Bucks County somewhere. Maybe it was Bristol, I don't really know. But what I know for sure was that it was down the street from the "Midway Inn" because it was where we spent most, if not all of our time.

It was just my mother, my little sister of 13 months younger and I. Why and how did we end up in this trailer park? Well, it was a step up from the car we lived in for a brief moment in time. Being so young, I really don't know how long we lived in it, but one night was bad enough. The story my mother told us was that she left my father in Connecticut, who was an abusive alcoholic. My father's side of the story, which I wasn't able to hear for many years later, was that my mom was a secretary at the police station, and was having an affair with one of the police officers. My mom did say that he punched a police officer and went to jail, so maybe in between those stories somewhere the truth lies. Over time everyone's memories fade and blur into other events and stories and you just never really know where the truth is. They each have their own truth and that's what matters most. Either way, she did leave him one day, drove to her parents house in PA and was rejected at the door with 2 very small kids in tow. My mother said that my grandmother advised her to drop us off at an orphanage or at the doorstep of some strangers and walk away. That she had made her bed and needed to lie in it. My mother refused to do that, and so my grandmother at some point bought us this trailer to live in.

I have realized over the years that abuse is in our DNA and it's also karmic. I know the things that I have gone through have had to be a part of some bigger plan God has for me. I have always felt like that since I was young. I just feel it in my heart. The abuse that I have endured, is a part of my roots, it's a part of me, it's in my blood and has been stored subconsciously and consciously in my body. It has interrupted and shaped my life dramatically.

I can't speak for my sister or anyone else in my family. At the time I have been writing this, we are actually not speaking. It's been years since we connected, which is not abnormal for our relationship. I know I have tried speaking to people on occasion of some of these events, and the conversations and their memories have been distorted over time. Some of them have no more recollection of the events where they previously had remembered somethings before. As time has gone by their memories have seem to fade away, washing away all of the things they wish to no longer see. I remember about a decade my mother and I had a heart to heart about many of these things to which we both cried and apologized. Me for being a reactive and unpredictable teenager, rebelling. Her apologizing for the abuse and doing only the best that she could at the time. I hold on to those conversations because now she seems to have no recollection of anything or admittance to anything that has gone wrong in the past. I will say that we are results of our environment, and things affect people differently. I have long since forgiven her, forgiven the other people that abused me, and most of forgiven myself.

I decided to rise above my abuse. I never wanted to be a victim. I had spent years as a child hating myself and wishing and wanting to die. I felt worthless, unloved and didn't want to feel the pain any longer. I was a pawn to use against my father by my mother for money. I was told I was a piece of crap. But I never wanted to live like a victim. I just never knew how not to be a victim until I grew into age, and decided to change it and learn that I actually had the power to change it. For this reason I could no longer have relationships with some friends and pretty much my entire family because when I changed and grew they didn't like it.

I stopped fitting into the mold they created for me. **This is my story, not theirs.**

The Midway Inn was a large maroon colored building on the outside with white trim. A nice size parking lot, surrounded by small neighborhood trailer parks. I have a skewed point of view from a 5 year old perspective, but I hated that place. I don't know if my mom had a job then, but we spent every waking and non waking moment at the bar. You see, nowadays if you brought children to a bar, you would be looked down upon, if they would even let you in. In the 80's there were real lax parenting rules and regulations, for which now you would end up straight in jail. Even back then I remember thinking at that young age how crazy it was that my mom was allowed to do these things. Spending all day and night at a bar, she flirted with random men. We would get change in quarters and play video games, or with the pool tables. We often got yelled at from the bartenders for playing with pool balls, or the sticks, thinking we would scuff up the felted tables. We were the only kids there, or any bar we frequented over those young years. It didn't even occur to me we were the only children until right this second.

We were skinny little girls with long dirty blonde hair. Me being about 4 or 5, that would make my sister 3 or 4 so we were young enough apparently that my mom wouldn't leave us home alone yet. So bringing us to the local bar would have to suffice for her to live her life. Because it was *her* life, I just happened to be a tagalong.

Going back to the trailer park during my college years brought back a lot of memories of the bar. I was doing one of my photography projects on the pain I went through and went to the old neighborhood to take pictures. It wasn't until later on in life did I realize that our trailer, where we lived at briefly, was actually right down the street from the bar. It just made me crazy because once dinner time hit, begging for food didn't help my case to leave the bar. I would eat chips or peanuts and then had to pass out asleep in the car when we only lived half a mile down the road.

I would take my mom's keys and fall asleep in the car. This was, what felt like, a nightly occurrence. I knew how late it was, or how close it was to closing when all the drunks would leave the bar, and would try to talk to me in the car. I never opened the door. Drunk people were always annoying and the men were all perverts. Although, that may have been because what was about to happen to me changed my view of the male gender. When I was photographing the area for my project I was so upset when I learned how close we lived to that bar. Why couldn't she just tear away from the bar to put us to bed? It was so close, we could have walked it ourselves. Looking at it from the adult perspective was really eye opening, realizing that as a child I had felt like we were in a completely different town.

I had spent so much time of my childhood in bars that I later became pretty good at pool. It was like my claim to fame. "I grew up in a bar, I better be good at it." We were never wanted at the bar. The bartenders hated us, as we would fight over the pool balls, gather up the blue chalk, and try to chalk all the sticks up. We would fight over all of it, my sister and I. The men at the bar hitting on my mother, who was and still is gorgeous, wouldn't want us there. In fact, our mother always ignored us, as if we did not exist to her.

We spent what felt like hours in her car. Who knew what the actual time was, but we would constantly walk in and out of the bar to ask her how much longer. "How much longer?" Whining. Constantly. We wouldn't get answers, but that never stopped us from trying. Eventually my mother would stumble into the car, and drive us home. I always faked sleeping so she would have to pick me up and put me to bed. The only sort of good physical contact I would ever get from her. It continued later on in life when I would literally fall out of my bed and make a loud noise so my mom would come upstairs and pick me up and put me back to bed. I did it every night when I knew she was home. Sometimes I would do it over and over again if she didn't come to my room. Maybe I wasn't loud enough for her to hear. Eventually, my mom put my sister and my beds together to try to prevent it. All I ever wanted was a loving touch from my mother. All I wanted was attention from her and to be loved.

One day I met a young girl, about the same age as me. She had lived upstairs at the Midway Inn. She claimed her dad owned the bar. It was a weekend, sunny day in the summer and we had ventured around the property. She took us upstairs at the Inn, walked the hallway, and played around the trash dumpster and in the few trees that were around the building. Then we went to the bus stop overhang which was this rickety old hut made out of wood, assuming it was made to be safe from the cold winter snow while waiting for the bus. I looked down and caught a glimpse of what would be my first pornographic magazine. I will never forget it, as I am sure every teenage boy can recall their first dirty mag. There it was, the girl and I brought it over to a clearing spot behind some trees in an effort to hide. We stared at every page, turning each page really slow. I remember looking at the men and being so freaked and totally grossed out. That is what a man looks like naked? We laughed at it in awe and disgust. As a five year old girl, seeing grown men naked in a pornography magazine is not the right way to start out life or a positive way of being introduced to sex. I have never gotten those images out of my head.

Although this was the start of my earliest memories, we didn't live there very long, less than a year. It was this very short period of time in which my childhood innocence was taken away and haunted me for close to 30 years. I think my mom tried to do something to keep us occupied, but it never worked. My mother adopted a dog from the pound, which lasted one night, because it had worms, and had to go back. Another dog we got, we tried to walk, a huge german shepherd and one foot out the door on a leash, and it dragged me until I had to let it go. We never saw it again. She tried but it always failed. Instead of pets I was always occupied by her alcoholic rants, physical, mental abuse or by the abuse I was about to endure and will share with you now.

Her response was to treat us the same way other people treated her. Or how she treated herself. It was with anger, hatred, resentment and no love at all.

I am assuming my mother eventually got a job, because our neighbors started babysitting us. They were a large family with older kids. Though we all had spent most of our time outdoors. One day they took us to Burger King in their excursion van. The older son decided to give me a piggyback ride out the side door of the van, and as soon as he stood up, my head went straight into the side of the door where a large protruding metal object went right into my forehead. Blood gushing everywhere, they brought me inside Burger King and I remember seeing the trail of blood leading towards the bathroom. An ambulance came, but they just bandaged me up, and we got our food and went back home. After that we pretty much were on our own because my mom didn't trust anyone to take care of us. At the age of 5 I became a grownup and had to babysit myself and my little sister.

It wasn't unheard of for a child of the 80s to just run around the neighborhoods by themselves. It was before predators were really talked about or feared. Everyone was in this fake world where everything was great, and no one liked to talk about bad things happening. Especially in their own backyard.

There were lots of kids in the trailer park neighborhood. Pretty much all older than us, a few of the same age. We would follow the older kids around, or play at the little fenced in playground. Which was almost always locked up. Why have a playground and then lock it up? I remember an older lady who lived on a street behind ours that lived in a beautiful trailer, it was well decorated, with floral prints, doilies, and nice photographs. She loved talking to all the kids, and giving us treats every now and then. She was either a mother of one of the kids, or a retired older lady. She was just so sweet and kind to all of us. I always felt safe walking by her house and often looked to see if any of the lights were on to know if she was home.

Another neighbor I spent time with was a large, overweight man that lived 2 doors down from us. He wasn't obese, but I do remember him being very big. In my mind, he was sweaty, wore glasses and suspenders. He spent all his time in a chair in his driveway, which was the front yard for our trailers. Being so young, we always followed the older kids around. I am assuming that is how I ended up being at his house the first time. Though, I remember him giving me candy and thinking that made me feel special. I was always a really shy child, as a result of being mentally and physically abused. It had forced me over the years to become very introverted, always staring at the ground and never ever talking. Ever. In fact, I had become so introverted that I stopped looking up from the ground for the rest of my childhood and most of my adulthood. Eventually, my back curved, my shoulders rolled inward and down and my back became twisted to the side in order to feel protected. Abuse does take physical forms in the body, in just very different ways. I believe it was created in my body because I look at pictures of me when I was young and I don't have the same posture issues as I did as an adult, and it is clearly visible on x-rays and the MRIs. The doctors call it Scoliosis. Later, I would learn that not only was my physical body showing signs from abuse in this lifetime, but also from trauma related to many past lives in addition to generational trauma, but maybe all of that is for a different book.

My previous abuse didn't exactly help me to be able to protect myself from what was about to happen.

All the kids were told to call him Uncle Bill, and so that's what I did.

He would call me over, and I would go to him. He was always outside, there was almost no way to escape him. He would give me candy and sweets, and I guess I felt like I had to do him a favor in return. He would pick me up and sit me on his lap. Almost like playing a kids game where your father would put you on his lap and pretend to be a pony galloping away. He would pull my shorts over to one side, and stick his large fingers up my private parts. Bouncing me up and down while molesting me and taking away all the innocence I had left in my small existence of a world. It happened on numerous occasions. For most of my life I didn't understand why I let it happen. But I also didn't know that I had a choice in the matter. I was taught that you listen to adults and I was already being abused so it didn't seem I was worthy of anything else but abuse. In fact, it was all I knew. It was normal to me.

My mom had a boyfriend who would often be drunk at our trailer at late hours of the night. I would be woken up to screaming, which is hard to ignore in such tight living quarters. One night I woke up and just stared out the crack of the door. He hit my mother, and she was screaming and crying. They both took turns throwing anything they could find at each other until everything we owned was broken on the kitchen floor. I must have fallen asleep on the floor because a little while later I awoke to my mother screaming at me, pulling my hair, dragging me to the kitchen to clean up the mess while she proceeded to pass out in bed as the sun started to rise. I will never forget that mess, and it seems like an odd thing to remember at such a young age. But there were broken dishes everywhere mixed in with tons of dirt from potted plants being thrown. To this day it was the hardest mess I ever had to clean up. I was scared to death if I hadn't had it cleaned up by the sun rising. It felt like it was straight out of one of those vacuum infomercials. One vacuum to clean it all. Broken glass, no problem. Dirt, food, spills, no problem. It will clean it all or you will have bruises all over our face. You will have cuts and marks up and own your arms, you will be kicked, punched and your hair will get pulled.

My mom seemed to have a problem with breaking dishes. To this day, I am convinced that it was passed down in my DNA because as an adult I often have broken so many dishes by accident that it just can't be a coincidence. I then started to buy backups and stopped buying anything expensive because it's not a matter of "if" it will break, but when. Thankfully, I have finally resolved that in my DNA because it doesn't happen any longer but conveniently my daughter often tells me of the broken dishes and the clumsiness that she seems to currently have as a result of being born from me. I'm hoping one day I can help her to resolve that as I was able to. I know it may seem ridiculous to think that you can pass down something like breaking dishes to your offspring but this is something you just can't ignore. It's so specific and obvious it would be ridiculous not to pay attention to it, in my eyes.

One day while in our trailer, the police knocked on the door. I remember being very scared and worried because I thought I had done something terrible. There were two uniformed police officers, which was very intimidating to a little kid who was always told police were "bad". They asked a few questions which I refused to answer. I just stared off into the distance as if they weren't there right in front of me of flesh and blood. They were either great officers for being able to tell something was wrong, or they already had information and just needed me to confirm it.

Almost a month has gone by since I tried to write this chapter. Once I got to the last paragraph I went through so much physical reawakening of trauma that it started affecting my daily life and I had to stop writing. Talking about the past made me relive it in a way that I was suppressing the whole time, though I thought I had healed it fully. That was wrong. It only uncovered what was hiding even deeper and had me relive and experience it all over again. All the emotions came back and included ones that I didn't know were hiding in my shadows. I felt like I had been there, again. I felt numb. It was happening to me all over again. I felt violated and I haven't even completed the story yet. I haven't been able to be intimate with my husband since I started writing this story. He would touch me and I would cringe with fear and disgust. A man I have been with and felt safe with for 18 years and all of a sudden my body started shutting down with just talking about a memory from 35 years ago. As a result of this we had to start going to marriage counseling and therapy.

It's amazing what happens to our body and our minds in the face of trauma. It was really interesting to me what also started happening to me in my physical body. I was noticing that as a result of what I was uncovering was directly affecting my physical body. I started to go inward again as if I was that small, young, lost little girl. There are so many layers to trauma and we have to peel them away, slowly, one at a time and only when we are ready to shed them.

So back to the story. The police came and asked my mom to leave my bedroom so I could talk to the officers. One was a lady, and one was a man. I just sat there on the day bed staring at a stuffed animal. I was scared of it, and didn't want the police to know. They tried really hard to get me to talk, but I just couldn't. The one officer caught on quickly. Maybe it's a part of their training again or they already had information. She asked me what was wrong, and I pointed to the stuffed teddy bear. I told her the bear was given to me by "Uncle Bill" and he told me that if I said what he did to me that the bear would tell him and he would harm my mother. I believed that, I really did think the bear was communicating to him. The officer looked at it, and removed it from the bedroom. I slowly started feeling more comfortable, realizing these were not bad people. The one officer asked me questions about every detail to which I just answered yes or no.

Do you know your neighbor Bill?

Yes. I replied.

Have you ever gone to his house?

Yes.

Did you ever go over there by yourself?

Yes.

Did you ever go over with other kids?

Yes.

Did you ever sit on his lap?

Yes.

Did he touch you?

Yes.

Did he touch anyone else?

Yes.

Can you show us where he touched you?

And there is where I froze. I just sat, frozen. The lady officer handed me a Barbie doll and asked me to show her where he touched me on the doll, as if it somehow resembled a 4 year old little girl. While this was going on I actually felt ashamed for being a tattle tale. What I was going to tell was going to cause pain. It was all my fault, and I thought that I was a terrible kid for telling on him. My mom is going to hate me and I am going to be in so much trouble. He is going to know what I told the officers. My family would be in big trouble. I believed the bear had powers over me. I believed it had cameras in its eyes, and told him what I was up to on a daily basis. At the time, I really thought it was real. You can tell a child anything and they will believe you because they have no reason not to.

I cried and cried and cried. I never saw Uncle Bill again. All of a sudden a mother's worst nightmare came true. All the rashes on my vagina and marks on my rear end now had a diagnosis that the doctors had no explanation for previously.

No one ever talked about it again. We moved shortly after to another house where I then started 1st grade and my sister went to Kindergarten. I wanted to know what happened when I got older. Did he ever go to jail? Did he pay for what he did to me? I found out later that the older kids testified and sent him to jail, only for a short period of time though. He ended up moving to Florida with his family, where he kept molesting children. He even got his own daughter pregnant. He spent time in and out of jail, but always went back to being a predator. It's unreal to me that people like this rarely spend time in jail. It's worse than any other offense I can think of. Being sexually molested as a child leaves an imprint in their mind and body that is hard to overcome. It can never be forgotten, no matter how hard you try to heal from it. Suppressing it is even worse, since you can't ever learn from it or grow as a person if you try to pretend it never happened in the first place. Suppressing it into your soul is only fuel for self hatred and a prison for your mind and body. It caused so much pain in my life. For a really long time. Until right now.

There was no worse thing on this planet that I had experienced and from that point on, I felt like I was completely alone. That experience shaped the way I looked at men, it shaped the way I interacted with every single person from that moment forward. There was a part of me that was stuck there at that time. It was, and remains still, my earliest memory of this life. A part of me that took many, many years to retrieve back into my energetic body was fragmented and needed a lot of work in order to bring it back to my soul and to be made whole again.

in child sex assaults

By David Barnett Jr.
and George Mattar
Courier Times Staff Writers

A Bristol Borough man and a Falls Township man have been arrested and charged in separate incidents with sexually molesting a number of children in the two towns, police revealed Tuesday.

Edward R. Torha, 62, of 102 Radcliffe St. in Bristol, faces charges involving an 11-year-old boy whom he allegedly molested at least three times since Labor Day, and faces additional charges of similar acts involving five other boys, ages 8 to 11, since January, borough police said.

William E. Underkofler, 43, of 9841 Lawson Drive, Pennwood Crossing Trailer Park in Falls, was charged Saturday with indecent assault on one boy and three girls, ages 4 to 6, according to Falls police records.

In the Bristol case, the victims were lured by gifts of cheap digital watches and ice cream from the retired U.S. Steel worker they knew as "Pappy," police said.

Police said the incidents came to light Friday after a woman acquaintance noticed the 11-year-old boy was "acting strangely." She advised the boy's parents she thought something was wrong.

This resulted in a father-son talk in which the boy — who had been afraid to tell his parents — told his father what had taken place, police said. The boy's father notified authorities.

Police said the boy had been lured by the man with the promise of frozen ice cones.

Police said three incidents took place: One Sept. 2 near the gazebo on Samuel Clift Drive, another in the man's room in the King George Hotel, and the third at the corner of Pond and Washington streets.

As a result of the information they received, police obtained a warrant and arrested Troha Saturday at his room at the hotel. He was charged with indecent assault and corrupting the morals of a minor.

He was arraigned before District Justice Jennie I. Pekarski, who ordered him held in Bucks County Prison in lieu of $50,000 bail pending a preliminary hearing.

On Tuesday, Detective Charles Favoroso and Officer Dominick DiRenzo — who described the recent alleged incidents with the 11-year-old boy as "just the tip of the iceberg" — were interviewing other reported victims and their friends and relatives as they continued their investigation.

They said they learned of the other victims as a result of their probe.

Police also believe other boys may have been involved and have asked other possible victims to contact them or call police headquarters, 788-7811, where all calls will be kept confidential.

In the Falls case, the sexual assaults allegedly took place between July and August and involved two 5-year-old girls, a 6-year-old girl and a 4-year-old boy, according to police records.

Underkofler was arraigned before District Justice Dominick Spadaccino and sent to the Bucks County Prison in lieu of $25,000 bail. A hearing date has not been set.

2

Sonic Youth

I saw petafiles in every man I ever met from that point on. Even in my own father who had never done anything to me. Once my mother left my father, I didn't remember seeing him again until I could remember around age 8 or 9. I feel like a chunk of my life has been temporarily erased by trauma and I have been trying to get it back ever since. By this age we had moved again and somehow he came to pick us up and take us to Vermont to spend time with his family up there. I never knew this man, and now I was alone with him and I was petrified. He had a dark maroon van, with the seats taken out of the back of it and a bed laid out so we could take naps during the long ride up north which was about 8 hours or so. My father was and still is a bit of an oddball and I mean that in a positive way because of the interesting way he walks and lives his life. He can never be copied or duplicated. Having a military background, he was always doing things efficiently. He brought a portable toilet so we had to use it in the van because he didn't want to pull over and waste time using the bathroom. I was always way too scared to use it in front of him, so I pretty much held it in until he was forced to stop for gas. Because of the abuse I had experienced it made me even more scared to be around men, and more especially while having my private parts exposed, even if it was just to use the bathroom in front of my own father. My nervous system was stuck in that constant state of trauma.

While in Vermont we stayed at our Uncle's house who also lived in a trailer. He was a quadriplegic and had no use of his body below his neck. He was able to move his arms, though he was not in control of movement of his hands. All of a result of a motorcycle accident when he was a teenager. He had figured out a way to play Nintendo with his knuckles and for that as a child he became my hero. He beat every level of Mario Brothers and Zelda, and I was in complete awe of him. He was the most kind hearted man I had ever met, and despite being handicapped, he still had a sense of happiness, one that I felt even as I watched him pass away many years later.

Our first few days there were spent painting a wheelchair ramp my dad had helped build for him. He used to use 2 pieces of wood and had to be pushed straight up a very steep incline. It was scary to say the least, especially for my grandmother or the aides that were the ones to usually help him in and out of his trailer. Eventually there was a very nice deck built with a wrap around ramp and the two planks were gone. We were in charge of staining it and although it wasn't much fun for little kids, I was happy just to be doing something. Later on as the sun started to go down, my dad decided he wanted pictures taken of him and his children. He kneeled down on the lawn and put me on his lap.

I had lost it on the inside. I barely said anything. I just had a terrified look on my face. I was reliving all the abuse, I was petrified. I thought it was going to happen all over again. Every time my Dad touched me, I would cringe, and it wasn't even his fault. He didn't even know the abuse had ever taken place. He didn't know of the abuse my mother had done to me. He was totally unaware.

He put his arm around me for the pictures and I started crying. It felt like I was unable to love or be loved after the molestation. Even by my own father, he never had a chance to be my father. I was damaged goods before I was even able to have a relationship with him. That was just not fair, to either of us. From that point on, every time I looked at that picture, I was reminded of the abuse and what I was thinking of at that very moment. My father's picture of me, and it was of me with pain in my eyes. You can see it all over my face. You can see me being so standoffish, and pushing him away from me. I can still remember the fear, and the awkwardness. You could read the terror all over my face, and it was captured in a photograph for which time would always stand still.

I recently looked into the statute of limitations, which is 30 years after the abused child turns 18. That would make me 53. I still have time. I tried to look up information about the man that molested me, my mother had given me his full name and the newspaper article about him being arrested but I couldn't find anything on the computer. I don't live in the town anymore, not even in the same state so it is unlikely that I am able to find public records from where I stand now. I tried contacting the government agencies and was assigned a lady to help me, but it's been months and I have yet to hear back. At this point I see no value in trying to seek and get revenge. My mom said all the children's parents in the neighborhood pleaded together. I am unsure what that means exactly and I don't think I will ever get any answers, especially the answers that I really would like to hear.. and I am finally ok with that.

When I was around 10 years old I started menstruating and was at a regularly scheduled pediatric check up. The doctor told my mom to leave the room so he could take a blood sample. He told me to drop my pants, I really didn't want to because at the time I had my period. I finally did it, and layed on the table. He said he could only take blood from the inside of my thigh and that I had to take off my underwear. I said no, and asked why he had to take it from there. I finally said I wanted my mom and I had to argue and yell for her to come into the room. She heard me because she was standing just outside the door. I whispered what happened in her ear and she asked him why it was necessary, but she immediately knew something was wrong with him. He then spouted off that I was going to die in 3 months and that the procedure had to be done the way he said because he was the "Doctor".

I left the office balling my eyes out, and my mom never took us back to another family doctor, ever. I remember witnessing the same doctor who had slapped my sister across the face for crying in the office at an earlier appointment. I had wondered why it took my mom so long to leave that office. I will never forget what it looked like. A nice white grand building. It was a far drive, through a very affluent area. Maybe a friend of the family. My mom never told me that I wasn't going to die. She just let me go on living. I went to school and told my friend what had happened, and she treated me differently after that. After a few months I had realized I wasn't going to die, nor did I contract some sort of disease. It sort of gave me an obsession with thinking I was always dying of something. In my mid twenties I sort of became a hypochondriac and I contributed this event to the manifestation of that within my mind.

From the trailer park, we had moved to a bigger place. A nice townhouse in a Jewish neighborhood. I remember that because it was brought up often. How we were the only ones with Christmas decorations up during the holidays. How our neighbors hate us because we were different. Yet she was the one who seemed to hate everyone else for not being like us. Never realizing they just didn't like us because of how my mother acted. Though it was less frequent during the short period of time we lived there, there were still issues. My mother ended up getting a better job and so when Christmas came that year we had lots of gifts to open. I will never forget that as a child who was always "needy" or never having *enough*. The presents that year made me forget about the reality that was around me or the past that I had come from in such a short period of time.

We had a den, which was filled with toys, and often spent time running around behind the houses and staying next door playing board games with the girl that was our age. We even had a pet turtle who had free rein of the house, and ate food with the cat. We often played with him outside until one day he ran away and we never saw him again. I learned later as an adult that turtles hibernate. So now I assumed that all he did was bury himself under a bush to hide until he was ready to emerge again. I had never known turtles did this until a friend's child had a turtle as a pet and I saw them bury him in a tupperware full of dirt and put him in the garage. This made me happy because as a child that lost a pet my mind immediately went to being eaten by another animal.

Hibernation was a much better way to be or to walk away as a child's pet, I thought.

I got all my favorite things for Christmas, a Pac Man record, a George Michael record, a Nash skateboard and a little toy horse and stable set. I loved horses. It must be my spirit animal, because I have no reason to like them, but they have always been in my heart growing up. Maybe it's just a girl thing though. It's a beautiful majestic animal and the closest thing to a unicorn. I was a young girl totally and completely obsessed with them.

Riding in the car as a child, I would block out what was my real life, and would stare out the window and pretend I was a horse following along the side of the road. I would make her jump over cars, go under signs, eat the grass at stop lights. That horse version of me would just prance and fly through the air all day. I would lose myself in that horse and believe that I was her. It was the only thing that made me forget the physical reality I was living in.

My mom was still seeing this guy from the trailer park that had often caused problems. In fact he had shown up causing more problems in the new house as well. Eventually, my mom started taking us to her work with her on the weekends, and we would end up being bored out of our minds. She tried babysitters again, and we ended up at a ladies house who wasn't very nice. I mean that with respect, as I don't know how else to paint the picture. She lived a few blocks away from us and we stayed there after school until our mom got home from work.

She was really mean, and strict. She had older kids, who sometimes played with us, but there was nothing to do at her house. Everything was in pristine condition. Everything had a place, and everything was in its place.

There was a large swordfish taxidermied on her wall right above a big piano. We were never allowed to touch the piano, and I thought that scary stuffed fish was watching my every move at all times. The babysitter also had a way of disciplining us that we weren't used to. If we got out of line, or if my sister and I ever fought, we would have to sit in the naughty chair in the kitchen, which was the worst. Other than that, the only other thing we were allowed to do was play with playing cards. So we often tried building houses of cards on her pool table. Pool table, there it is again. A pattern that should not be ignored.

I always felt the fish was watching my every move. It felt similar to that stuffed bear that was waiting for me to tattle tail. It never felt comfortable there, and there was no love in that house. I hated being there, though it was better than being home alone. At least we were fed.

One day, my mom ran to the house, I don't know why she didn't drive over. But she came to the door crying, and told the babysitter to call the police. There was blood pouring down her face going everywhere. Trent was his name, and he had broken her nose. It was repeated numerous times in my mom's life. Punching a woman's face so hard that you break her nose..That's a poor excuse for a man, and there were more than one of those in our lives.

Trent was chasing her down the street trying to get inside. We were all petrified, until the lady told him she had called the police and you could hear sirens quickly approaching. I wish he was out of our lives at that point, but he wasn't the one that didn't exist anymore. For whatever reason, we never saw that babysitter again. We ended up moving shortly after that incident. According to my mother and grandmother, there was a lawsuit pending with our neighbor over our gutters. Our town house was on the top of a steep hill, and apparently the neighbors didn't like that the gutter we shared drained onto their lawn. Not by our fault though, it was based on the law of gravity, and their house was below ours. I don't know why grown adults couldn't just resolve the issue and make the gutter longer and drain to the street. I guess it's easier to pay lawyers and complain about stuff instead of resolving it through communication.

Maybe it was just a way for them to try to get us out of the area. Either way, it ended up working ,and we moved yet again to another town, to another school. My third school in the same amount of years, I was starting to fall behind. Each school district had their curriculums, and every time we moved, I went to a different district. As a result, I didn't learn things properly because they were taught at different times of the year. Sometimes I moved in the middle of the school year which made things even harder on me, especially socially. I didn't learn how to tell time, how to do math correctly, and the biggest problem I had was with reading. Spelling was also a problem, but I quickly learned how to cheat on the spelling tests, and eventually the multiplication tests. I hated being called out for being so slow. During reading time, we were in groups, and we had to close our books when we were done reading the story. It quickly turned into a race to see who could finish reading first. I was always last and was being made fun of, so I eventually started closing my book not finishing the reading as I turned the pages to the end of the story.

The spelling tests were always hung up, and out of embarrassment, I eventually started writing the words on my hand, or on small pieces of paper and hiding them. I learned that trick from a fellow student. That fellow student got caught cheating and reprimanded and so I was too afraid to cheat again and figured out other ways to learn. I did eventually get really good at math, specifically Algebra, and even became a tutor to fellow students in college, but at the time, I had missed learning multiplication because in one school it was taught later, and the school I moved to had already learned it. It was a very troubling transition for me and further moved me down the rabbit hole as a young, shy kid terrified of speaking up or having attention placed on me, because getting any sort of attention meant terrible things were going to happen.

For math, we were not allowed to go to the next unit of learning until we passed the "Quiz". Every week we were asked times tables until one by one each student moved on. I was one of the last people left, me and Bobby who was a bright red headed kid who always wore Guns and Roses t-shirts. I didn't want to be the last one. Everyone made fun of him because he smelled, and probably came from a poor family as well, but he was always a nice kid, and actually got me big into metal music later on. I ended up cheating to pass the quiz, and was so relieved when it was all over. I had felt so bad about cheating that school year that it started to make me try to work much harder in school. I had a really hard time reading, it took me a really long time to read even one sentence, and then trying to retain the knowledge was even harder. It was only until I was an adult and actively tried working harder and reading a lot more did my brain get better at reading and retaining much more. It's a muscle as well, the more I work it, the stronger it gets.

Next we ended up in Langhorne, PA and stayed there until I graduated high school. I ended up going to another elementary school, my 4th one because they decided to split up the property lines for who went to which school. Transitioning from Oliver Heckman to Herbert Hoover wasn't so bad. Some of the same kids went with me, and so it wasn't done alone.

The most memorable moments for me for those years were of me being so traumatized that I was unable to speak or use my voice at all. All the abuse had taken its toll on me as a child, physically, emotionally and mentally. One time I had to go to the bathroom after lunch, but we were in lines being directed to the school store before we were allowed to make our way back to the classrooms. I had to pee so bad, and was so afraid of speaking up and asking the teacher if I could go that I ended up peeing my pants in the hallway as everyone stared at me. I just stood there frozen in space. At that point I think I was in 4th or 5th grade. Way too old to be peeing my pants, and it happened more than once at that school. On top of all that I was also getting terrible nosebleeds. Almost every day during a certain time of the year I had them at school throughout the day. I would always be sent to the nurse, and just sat there in the hallway with my nose up in the air with a bunch of paper towels. We tried humidifiers at home, but I would get them in the middle of the night in the dead of my sleep. I would wake up to the taste of the blood going from my nose to the back of my throat. Tasting blood is not something you can ever forget.

I started sleeping with a wet washcloth on my face, because it was just a matter of *when* the blood would start gushing, not *if*. My mom didn't take me to the doctors for it because of the problems I had mentioned earlier. We just couldn't trust them. The weekends had a sort of regularity to them by that point. My mom would take us to the convenience store for junk food and candy as dinner, and then to the West Coast Video where I would pick out a number of scary horror movies to rent. She would take me home, and say she was going grocery shopping. That was a Friday, and I wouldn't see her again till either Sunday night or Monday morning where she would come home, shower and change her clothes for work and leave.

I would stay up all night with the lights turned off, watching Nightmare on Elm street, or some other B rated scary movies, until all my candy and soda was gone and I would pass out on the brown, fake leather couch. Only to wake up in the early morning hours and drag myself to my bedroom upstairs. Sometimes I would go outside and play with the kids in our neighborhood. We would play manhunt. We would all walk up to Brothers Pizza and pitch in for a large pizza pie. We would walk the backway to the plaza in hopes to catch a glimpse of the horse that was kept in a neighboring backyard. No one ever cared that my mom was never home. I don't know if they even ever knew. It wasn't a big deal back then though. We were "latchkey" kids, and somehow it translated to me raising myself. It really wasn't that abnormal for kids to be out playing for hours with no parents at the house to keep track of us. That was a normal family living in the 80s and 90s.

By Sunday, all my candy and soda had been gone, and I would be so hungry and feel so lonely. I used to stare out the large bay window which had the perfect view of the beginning of the housing development. It would be dark, and I would just stare out the window looking for headlights of passing cars turning onto our main road. I would say to myself, God, let this be her. But it never was. It was the same thing every weekend. Gone to go "shopping" but not coming back. When she did end up coming home, it was never with groceries. When I started questioning her about it because by the time the weekend was over, I was starving, she then started producing a bag of boxed items from the trunk of her car. The first time I realized right away that there was nothing refrigerated, no milk, eggs or juice, and once I looked at the receipt, I realized it was because it was from a trip she had made days earlier. Maybe on her way out to wherever she was going at the start of the weekend. It was always one or two bags of items, hardly enough food for 3 people to live off of. And every time we did end up having groceries in the house, I would literally eat all of it. If it were a box of fruit roll ups, I would eat the entire box in 5 minutes. I was in survival mode and didn't know when I would get food next. There was no sort of regularity or stability in my life. As a kid, you need these things to feel safe and to feel like you are taken care of. There was zero stability, something that still affects me as a grown adult today.

I was grateful for the free lunches at school provided because of the income status and our family size. At home, we usually had boxed cake mix and ice tea mix, and frozen steak ums' . Those were the staples in our house. I learned how to cook for myself, and for treats, I would take the ice tea mix, and drop little droplets of water in the can. The result was a tea mix formed of a ball of hard/wet-ness that I would then pick up and drop into my mouth and have it slowly melt away.

It was no wonder that half my mouth was filled with cavities by age 9 or 10 when my mom finally brought me to a dentist. Most kids dislike the dentist but I especially hated it as a child. She would drop me off, leave me there where they would try to numb my mouth after me taking loads of antibiotics because of my heart murmur. The numbing never worked right. The parts that were numb were always the parts not being worked on, or it wasn't enough novocaine to do any good at all. Something that I didn't realize until later when I learned about Ehlers Danlos Syndrom that runs in my family, to which this is a symptom of. The biggest problem I find with families today is that they hide health issues from themselves and each other. This could have helped me growing up, and when I had kids and concerns about my body later on in life. Instead I had to suffer because it wasn't known or talked about. I wasn't ever able to swallow pills for some reason, so I had to take chewables for the heart murmur. This transferred into handfuls of pills I had to break up to chew. It was an absolute nightmare. I had to start chewing the pills like an hour before the appointment, but it would take me so long to eat them, and wash down that gross chalky substance that it would take me an hour just to finish them all. I wish I could say that led to the start of my mother leaving me at places, but it wasn't the start of it. I would have to wait there for hours after the procedures until my mom would pick me back up. A trend that didn't go away in my childhood. Being left behind, and forgotten was a regular occurrence and became the norm.

One of the most memorable times was when I went to an after school function in Elementary school, maybe 4/5th grade, not sure whose idea it was since I never had any friends, but it was at the Palace skating rink which I have taken my kids to as well as its still around and thriving still to this day. The function was run by the PTA and all the parents would drop off the kids, we would skate around for hours, eating pizza, soda and then at the end of the night, you would get picked up by your parents or guardians. Except me. I waited and waited.

It was the PTAs job to wait with the kids until they all got picked up, but my mom didn't come for me when it was over. I told the patient mother to just leave me there because eventually I knew I would end up figuring out something on my own. (Back then there were no cell phones.) Somehow I think my life might be a whole lot different had I had one cell phone. Anyone would be just a few numbers away. They tried to call my mother, over and over. Left messages on the early 80's tape recorded answering machine. No answer. No call back. Nothing.

What felt like hours later, in my small child mind, my mom finally showed up. All the kids had gone home. The other parents and volunteers left as the sun was now sleeping and the sky was only lit up with bright street lamps. She sped through the parking lot, giving the nice lady a dirty look as if she was inconvenienced by having to pick me up. Yelling at me to get in the car, I quickly obliged. I could tell she was obviously intoxicated, and was prepared to brace myself for the long, uncomfortable ride home. Something that also was not foreign to me was getting in a car while the driver was intoxicated.

Palace Skating rink was about halfway to the City of Philadelphia from where I grew up being located on Roosevelt Boulevard. As you get closer to the city from the north east driving south, you end up on this large highway type of road. It's about 6 lanes going each way. 3 Lanes then a divider made up of a large grass plot with some trees, and then another 3 lanes. Double that going into the opposite direction and you can see what a cluster the driving is around that area. My mom pulled out of the skating rink parking lot which seemed like a Cruella De Vil reenactment, turned left and ended up going down the 2nd row of opposing traffic. I was holding on, and once I realized there were headlights headed straight for us, I started screaming at her that she was going the wrong way. Cars honking, swerving left and right trying to avoid my drunk driving mother with me in the backseat with no seatbelts on. Swerving back and forth, back and forth, until she finally drove up onto the grassy medium, and then drove the car over bumps and bushes, almost hitting a tree until we finally made it to the other side going in the correct direction and flow of traffic. I really thought that was going to be the end. It wasn't.

We did make it home safely, and I believe that was the real beginning of when I started to hate my mother and wished for her to die. I started to realize at that point that my mother was a bit different then all the others. I saw all the other kids' parents come pick them up, or better yet, stay with them and have fun and realize my mother was not at all like any of them. Once I realized what a real mother "looked" and "acted" like, I started with my hatred, anger and resentment. I started hating myself even more, I started hating life, and all I wanted was to die. That's a bit much for a 5th grader to have to think about. Having my daughter at the same exact age now as I was back then really puts it into perspective. Not a day goes by that I don't think about what is best for my daughter. I can't ever imagine thinking about anything but what is best for both my kids. As a child I was never allowed to go to another PTA event again after that incident. I was banned for good reason. That fueled me to be on the PTA at my daughters school and eventually volunteering in her 3rd and 4th grade classrooms. I needed to totally change and reverse that pattern of energy for my own kids.

I don't know what happened to her around that time, maybe she just started hanging with the wrong people, at the wrong bars, but it just went even more downhill from there. When I was in about 6th grade I really started becoming a parent, not just to myself but then to my own mother. It may have been earlier, but at this point, I was in full on parent mode already. I had to wake my mom up for work every morning at around 5:30am. I would hear her alarm going off through both our bedroom doors and the buzzer had no sign of ending until I personally turned it off. I would go in, hit snooze at which point I would try to tell her to wake up. It didn't always work, but then she would mumble out of the corner of her mouth to make her coffee. I had to learn through trial and error a few times because if it wasn't to her liking then I would get scolded. 5 cups of water turned out to be 4 scoops of coffee with the special little scoop that came with each can. If it was too watered down, she wouldn't drink it, tell me I couldn't do anything right and would make me do it all over again, or worse, dump it and have to remake it herself. That made me feel even more inadequate.

The coffee brewing smell wouldn't always work, but it worked more often than not for a while. I would have to wake her up several times before she ever actually made it to the shower. I honestly don't know how she kept that one job for so many years. I wouldn't have believed it if it weren't for a plaque they gave her for the 10 year anniversary of being there.

3

Kerplunk

Eventually, around the age of 11 she started making me drive her car for her when she was out of cigarettes and was too hungover to go to the store to buy them herself. Now remember, for those of you not born in the late 70's, maybe even the early 80's, no one cared who bought cigarettes back then. Can you believe it?! Now they certainly gave me a look when I drove up in my mom's blue grand prix and walked in and asked for cigarettes, by that time she had traded in her black Camaro sadly. My mom had a reputation to say the least and the lady that worked there knew my mom from hanging out at the bars, and for a while, my mom had me pay by writing a check. What a long way the world has come since then. Eventually, I stopped getting asked who the cigarettes were for, as if I was always telling the truth. "2 packs of Camel Lights." It wasn't long before my mom made me drive to other places for her as well. I was 11 and had no license or business behind the wheel of a car and yet I really didn't have a choice, at least that's the way it felt to me.

By about 7th grade, the physical abuse I received from her started to end as I decided to start fighting back. I will never forget her grabbing my hair, pulling me down to the floor to start kicking me with her heels, and digging her sharp nails into my arm, when I decided I was just too big. I had legs too, and I started to fight back. She really put up a good fight that day, as I was backed into a corner, but once I got my legs out in front of me, I just started kicking and closed my eyes, and just cursed until I had no life left in me. She retreated and never put her hands on me again. I haven't talked much about the physical abuse from her yet.

As bad as it was, I think the mental abuse hurt a lot more. Anyone that has gone through similar situations may also agree with me. Maybe not, I can't really speak for other people. We all take things so differently. But for me, the mental abuse hurt me on a whole other deeper level, it hurt my soul to the core.

Growing up, I always had some sort of markings on my body. No one ever questioned it because we were kids. Young kids get hurt, they play outside, climb trees, play with kittens, fight with siblings...there was always an excuse for it. At one point the physical abuse was so bad that my arms were covered with scabs. One day I ended up in the emergency room because my eye started bleeding out of the corner where the tear ducts were. The doctors had no idea why I would be bleeding from there, blood streaming down my cheek. Something I still think about to this day. I have had some very interesting ailments that have had no explanations by doctors and as I continue to connect with the healer part of me that can work with energy, I am starting to wonder if they are all some sort of metaphysical manifestation of the power I have that lay dormant. The doctors looked at my arms, and ran some tests. They questioned why I had so many scratches and my mom said we had a litter of kittens that we were taking care of, which was a lie. As I lay there in the ER room, the doctor started conversing with my mother about possibly giving me a blood transfusion because I had lost so much blood from all these issues including the repeated nosebleeds. Who knows what it was, I am sure my body was in terrible shape from not eating regular food, or for not taking in as many calories as I should have been taking in at that young age. For whatever reason, I didn't end up needing..or shall I say, I never ended up getting one. I question it because if it came down to what was necessary for health VS. cost of procedures, I would have to just risk it. It always came down to a money thing. We were broke and didn't have health insurance. The only money we had was for beer and cigarettes. It just turned out that my grandparents were caring enough to buy that townhouse and let us live in it. We had no free health care back then, at least that's what I was told, though we had food stamps. My mom had a great job, I never knew what happened to her money. She did eventually get child support after years of going in and out of court to fight my dad. I am thankful though for not getting that blood transfusion. Back then, they didn't test blood for diseases that they do now.

My mom did a lot of drinking and driving. It was not abnormal to have a 6 pack in the front passengers side either. My mother eventually had so many DUIs that they took her license away. She was still drinking however, and still went out to bars. She drove sometimes, but there were other times that a friend would pick her up. It was one of these nights when a boyfriend had picked her up, and we didn't see her for the rest of the night. By then, we had had every phone number for all the local bars right next to the telephone that hung on the wall. If we had an emergency we were to try to locate our mother at any of these various places of alcohol consumption. I often tried calling them to find out when she would be home, never having any real emergencies. But eventually either the bartenders were a bunch of assholes, or my mom pretended not to be at any of them.

One night I actually got a phone call to the house, at early hours of the AM. Not remembering if it was a weekend or weekday, not that it mattered. There were often days I would have to drag myself to school, only to pass out on the desk from having to have stayed up all night from my mom's screaming rants, or fights with random men that would drop her off. This night was different though. I answered it, not remembering if it rang over and over until I dragged myself down the stairs to end the annoyance, but either way it was a surprise on the other end. My mother had called from St. Mary's hospital and needed me to pick her up. To this day I have no idea what happened. But I was given a location, which happened to be directly across from the Junior High school, and I was told to take the car, and to fetch her at the entrance at the main street. It was a far walk, and still dark out, as the sun just started to inch its way around the globe. I happened to see her body in a hospital gown, sitting on the curb smoking while being blinded from the bright headlights of the car. She had obviously had a real rough night of partying, I could see it in her eyes. I never said a word, and neither did she. How sureal of a night, being forced to become a grownup at a mere age of 12 having to pick up your mother from a hospital that looked like she had escaped from instead of being discharged. She must have felt so pathetic herself because she wouldn't even wait at the door of the hospital. It was probably a quarter mile walk of shame to that curb. Maybe it was simply because I was picking her up or maybe she just walked out against the better judgement of the doctors. I will never know. I wish I knew the pain my mother was going through. I wish she didn't run away from her problems or hide them. I can wish and wish for things to be different but the fact still remains. I asked for this life on a spiritual level. I will say this though for everyone reading. Do not think that running away, hiding, blaming, ignoring or denying your problems and pain will ever make it go away.

4

Sick Of It All

As I started to get older I started to feel more in control of things. Nothing really important of course, but I started to try to find my place in life. I started really rebelling. Through some friends at school, I found Punk Rock and Hardcore music. I started stealing my mom's cigarettes, stealing money from her purse, and always using her car while she laid totally passed out in bed from her hangovers. All the cash she kept in her purse was usually small bills, but in no sort of order. As you can imagine from the wreck of her life, her purse reflected the same. She never knew how much money was in her purse. So I naturally just started taking some. Not all of it, just enough to try to buy some food after school or on weekends when I needed to eat. Maybe enough to try to catch a movie or go to the mall. It's not like it was tons of money, though I am not condoning it either. There are many things I was ashamed of during the first half of my life, but when you're in survival mode, it doesn't really seem all that bad. Not that I even thought it was wrong at that point. I didn't have a great role model for those types of things. As I got older I really had to forgive myself for all the terrible things I did, regardless of why I did them, they still were not the right way to be. Once you are aware enough to know and feel the difference one small thing you do to another person you have no choice but to believe in karma and cause and effect and to try to rectify every single thing you have done to another into something a lot more positive.

After the era of writing checks, came the MAC card. A term that I have used recently by mistake at a gas station to which the young teenage boy gave me an odd look and asked what that meant. I said it 2 more times as if it would make him understand better, but it didn't until I remembered they don't use that term anymore. Boy did I sure age myself that day. A MAC card, or "Money Access Card" was the pre Debit check card or known now as the ATM. You couldn't use it at the stores, but you could go to a machine that had the MAC logo on it and withdraw cash from it that came out of your checking account. Same principle that still is used today, though that was the beginning stages of it. If my mom had no money in her purse for cigarettes, which she would direct me to go hunting for, I would have to take the card, use her PIN number and take out money to buy the cigarettes. Now, I have started learning some tricks. She would make me print out a receipt from the machine which would indicate how much you withdrew, and how much was left in the checking account. Forget a savings account, we lived check to check. Now, I would take out a 20 dollar bill, and then do the whole transaction all over again and give her the later receipt. She never knew the difference. She was so oblivious to everything going on around her except for her own self pity, that I could have gotten away with anything.

It's funny now that I think of it because later my mom had gotten a credit card in my name, and told us to buy Christmas presents with it and she said she would pay the bill. My sister and I went on spending and as the bills rolled in, my mom said she had no money to pay them. I spent years trying to pay that credit card off until I was done with college and it went into collections and they harassed me every day over the phone. My husband was so sick of the phone calls that he ended up paying the bill. It came back to me. It always does. Through our marriage credit cards became a real problem and once we divorced we had a ridiculous amount of debt. I finally fully resolved the energy behind that as well because I am debt free and plan to be, despite having a credit card in my name still. Just for emergencies.

Around 12 years old, I started spending a lot of time out of the house. Having graduated from the games played in the neighborhood of manhunt, the boys started all playing football in the field that the town-houses surrounded. The girls started liking boys, and I was just trying to survive and forget about my home life. This was when I finally started to make friends at school, and during the school year, I would stay after school until the late buses would line up at the end of the day to take all the athletes home after the school sports programs. Our lockers were alphabetically and the girl next to me, being at a different school pre-viously since a few elementary schools combined into one school that made up the junior high. Not having any knowledge of the names they used to call me, the girl whose locker was next to mine fastly became my friend. She acted way more mature than I did, and she sure taught me a lot about boys. I wasn't really interested in them, even just having had my first "french kiss" that previous summer from a neighborhood boy my age with a super handsome older brother. She let me follow her around like a lost puppy dog for months. She talked to me about boys, sex, periods, she cursed and had great.."big" hair and wore lots of makeup. I was in awe of her, and so thankful for her to just talk to me. She must have been popular in her school, because she quickly became popular with the "cool" kids from my previous school, and all of a sud-den I found myself trying to tag along with a lot of them. Back in ele-mentary school during lunch one day I had written the group of them a note, asking desperately if I could sit with them instead of by myself. I was so embarrassed that I had actually given it to them, that when they said I could go sit with them, I was mortified and wanted to die so bad that I was frozen and couldn't move to go sit with them. By junior high I wasn't as frozen inside of my body.

Noelle showed me that having boys like you was really cool. I fol-lowed her around, staying after school together, and we wandered around the sports fields looking for boys to catch our attention. When we got bored, we would wander the halls, go into the bathrooms and just talk about boys. I didn't care what we did as long as it involved me staying as far away from the nightmare that was my homelife. Not that it mattered anyway since we were latchkey kids, my mom didn't get home till around 5 anyway, that's only if she came home straight from work which wasn't often. Just the thought of me being in the house was enough to make me crazy, so I tried as hard as I could to stay away from it.

One day I came home after being at school from one of the late buses, and when I walked to the door, I saw something sitting on the steps. When I got closer, I realized it was a huge vase which turned out to be 60 carnations with a handwritten letter in a frame asking for a date with me. I had no clue who it was from, and I looked around and saw no cars, or anybody lurking around. I picked them up and walked inside. I noticed later that it had a name written in a nicely cursive style of writing. The next day, I ran into him and politely declined his advancement towards me. He was 2 years older than me which is a bit of a big difference when youre talking about me being 12 and him around 14 or 15. He was athletic, attractive, popular and Italian. I didn't have anything against him, and I don't think I even really had a "type" but I had a huge crush on a boy in my class named Omar. Omar was the one who really introduced me to music. Music ended up being the ONE thing that really saved my life, and I do think that I owe it to him. Omar had no interest in me, or in anything else other than his skateboard, but that didn't mean that I didn't try. He agreed to take me to the 6th grade Dance, for which he oddly got me a broccoli and cauliflower corsage, which I loved and may have asked for but can't remember, but as soon as the night was over, he quickly ran off with his friends. With skateboards in hand, they went off and left me while I went out with some other group of friends to the Ground Round for dinner being the only one dateless for the rest of the evening. Regardless of that being years earlier I still had a crush on Omar and I still had no interest in Jim. A week or two later, I opened up my locker with a scream as a bunch of things jumped out at me in horror. It wasn't anything horrific, in fact quite sweet. A number of stuffed animals and things that were pink or red, fluffy or covered in hearts. All things you would find at the local CVS during Valentine's day. It was sweet, yet I still wasn't interested in him. Obviously it was Jim, and he took credit for it rightly so. I still have no idea how he did it, but maybe it's better to be left to magic. Either way, he spent months, a total of about 3 months, begging for me to go out on a date with him. I had no idea what he saw in me. I asked him if I went out with him, would he agree to finally leave me alone, to which he agreed. Sadly, I don't remember the actual date we went on, I vaguely remember dinner but I am sure it was nice and romantic. He was very romantic, always concerned with trying to live the perfect dreamlike movie. Carefully trying to reenact a classic love scene to make me fall head over heels in love with him...which ended up happening. He was always caring, genuine and I felt like he really, really loved me. I spent every waking moment with him, and quickly started to be popular because he was 2 grades above me and popular himself. I started making new friends which were his, but really never felt comfortable with them. They were all super rich kids with nice clothes, huge houses, and attitudes to match in my opinion at the time. The area we lived in was a very wealthy school district since it was perfectly located 30 min from Philadelphia and about an hour ½ from NYC. I, on the other hand, was poor despite living in a nicer type of townhouse. The only clothes I had were the ones my grandma would buy for me, or clothes I borrowed from friends. It was still a few years before I was able to work to be able to buy my own things.

Jim was like a dream come true. He had a much younger brother, who when we weren't fighting, I would play with, or ask him to do things for me. He had an older sister who was either just out of high school or beginning college. We hardly ever saw her, as she was into her studies and never left her room, or out with her girlfriends. Jim's parents were never home either, as they both had jobs and worked long hours. Not that it mattered anyway because Jim and his older sister were more than capable of taking care of the younger brother. Jim played sports after school, so he quickly became a magnet to me. After school I would take the bus to his house, and then would beg for his mom or sister to drive me home at night. My mom quickly became jealous of Jim, and tried to make us end the relationship, but Jim, in his ever so prince charming ways, ended up winning her over in a huge way. He always listened to her, and did things for her until he won her over.

Around that age, my dad tried suing my mother for custody, which really went on for years, but it never concerned me until this particular age. I was 13 and the courts wanted me to choose who to live with. At that age, apparently the judge thinks I can make a rational decision. It's an interesting choice to place upon a teenager. I am 13, I finally have some friends and to top it off, I have a boyfriend that I love and loves me. I can pick to stay here in PA, or I can pick to live with my Dad, who I had only remembered a few times, who traveled around the world because he was on active duty. It was an easy choice for me. I don't care how much physical and mental abuse this lady who called herself my mother made me endure. I wasn't about to go globe trotting with a man I didn't even know. A man, by all accounts of my mother, was an abuser, drug addict, mean, nasty, horrible man who would never let me eat candy. Serious priority issues at age 13. I really don't know if my dad knew of the abuse at that age, but I know he really did love us. I also think that he would have done anything to not give her any of his money that he worked his ass off for. I later found out that my mom used the settlement of child support money for breast implants. I was so pissed when she told me later on, because during those years as I hit puberty and started growing into my own body, I was sure I was going to get her nice voluptuous breasts.

Having had the court date over and done with, testifying in court in front of both my parents that I choose to stay with my mother....the damage was done, and I could leave it behind now.

5

Quicksand

Jim was my rock and was always there for me. Being older than me, I guess he was around 16 by then and it was only a matter of time before he started pressuring me into what every teenage boy wants......sex.

A good number of months into our relationship and he started asking about it. I was a virgin, or at least in the normal sense I was a virgin, even though my innocence had been taken away at age 5. Sex was a very foreign thing to me, even though I had had numerous experiences "around" sexuality. All I knew about sex, was what I had learned about being molested, a porno magazine and what I had seen in all the horror movies I had watched on VHS. There was lots of sex in them. Lots of naked women running from various means of being murdered or mutilated. Always women. Insert eye roll here.

I was very fond of the female body, and often had weird sensations that arose in my private area when seeing people make out on TV or nude women. I guess that was the sure sign of hitting puberty and getting to know the reason for all these various body parts. After all, it was just for pleasure right? Nothing wrong with that. I was still deathly afraid of having actual intercourse. All the kids were starting to talk about it, though I doubt any of them ever actually had done it at that age. I can say that now because throughout the rest of my life when the conversation had come up about losing our virginity, and I speak off my age of being only 13, people make dramatic looks in my direction. So it must not have been the norm at the time...but again, he was older than I. I was really set on waiting after being together for 1 full year before taking that step but that still didn't keep him from asking me, and at 8 months, I finally caved in. Not that it mattered really, because we had already done absolutely everything besides sex by that point.

I befriended a new neighbor that moved in across the street named Megan. She had a younger brother and an older sister who had huge hair, and was into bands like Depeche Mode, the Cure and some other hair metal bands. I thought they were super cool, and glad that someone was so close. Megan was still a year older than me, so it worked out real well. I actually don't remember anything about her mom, but her father worked at an ice cream distributor and their house was constantly stocked full of it. It wasn't ice cream with milk, but it was in popsicle form, and was made with fresh fruits, as you could see chunks of what once was the actual fruit. We always tried to stay out of his hair, because he seemed to really dislike kids...and he actually became a big problem. Rather, we were the problem, I'm sure.

Megan, who had relocated from Phoenix Arizona, and I were close, though she made her own friends at school. She was what I considered to be my best friend. I had another friend in my neighborhood named Courtney but once I started hanging out with "Cool" Noelle, I dropped her quickly. She was nice and all, but I never felt comfortable at her house. She would beg me to come over, her house was really boring, and her mom made me uncomfortable. Maybe because she was "normal." I spent a lot of time with Megan, and we often went to the movies, the mall or to a religious after school program called "Mountaineers" on Thursday nights. Our parents were supposed to take turns picking us up and dropping us off, but it never worked out on my end. My mom did it a few times, and after being left there so many times, we had to eventually turn to Megan's elderly grandfather who probably should have stopped driving years earlier. It became so one sided that I eventually just had to stop going. It was for the better anyway because all I did while I was there was cause problems. I was "that" kid, who made fun of the teachers, constantly interrupted them, questioned God, and the bullcrap I thought they were feeding me. I know now that it was all for attention. I mean, why else would I act up? I started to act like that in school as well during this time, and had many out of school suspensions and ISS. (In School Suspensions) That was when I really started to just give up, I think. I acted up in school, when I wasn't passed out with my head on the desk, which was more often than not. Remember, I was being a parent to my own mother and little sister at this age. I barely ever slept, let alone did any homework. Anything having to do with reading, and I wouldn't be able to get through a chapter in one night. I never had a chance to catch up, no matter how desperately hard I tried at the time.

I had a Spanish 2 teacher, who must have been in her first or second year of teaching. I felt really bad for her because I walked all over her, every week. She had terror in her eyes every time she saw me, and I used that to my advantage. She was the reason for most of my suspensions. She was weak and unconfident in herself, and I saw right through it and took advantage of it, not consciously of course. I became some sort of class clown and constantly interrupted her to tell jokes, or to make fun of her. She would try to get me to stop, but it egged me on. I would curse at her and scream at her until she picked up the phone to call the principal. Then that was the indication that I had to walk my butt down to the principal's office. Which never did anything. They never tried to get to the real route of the problem, which wasn't me acting up, it was my home life. My mom never knew I was suspended, so it didn't matter what happened to me. In fact, it only fueled me to rebel more. Back then we were supposed to get a notice or tests signed by a parent. I brought a test home once for my mom to sign and when I returned it to the teacher, she accused me of forging it. My mom was hungover when she wrote it so all it was was a scribble, like a wavy line. After being accused of forgery, I had decided to just forge her handwriting for the rest of my school career. She never saw any report cards, tests or and school suspension letters because I was the parent with the appropriate signature.

Once Jim and I had been intimate with each other I confided with Megan. That seemed like a great thing to talk about with my best friend, but I could not have been more wrong at the time. I was sitting real nice and comfortable with my friends at school, my serious relationship with my boyfriend, and a routine of my life back home. But that was about to change. I walked into school one day and some older kids started making fun of me. Asking how it felt to have sex. I was called gross, disgusting, and then I was labeled a slut. Apparently Megan had decided to be a loudmouth and blab to everyone what I had confided to her in secrecy. She denied it of course, but I had not talked to anyone else, and boys didn't exactly brag about that sort of thing, or at least in a negative way. Besides it was all the kids in her grade level which isn't mine and wasn't Jims because he was 2 grades above me and she was only 1.

It was so bad, and humiliating that I started skipping school. I kept my distance from Jim, and stopped talking to Megan. Megan and I had been through alot of stuff. We had partied together a lot, and there were lots of secrets that she kept but this was just too much of a line that had been crossed.

Since my mom was never home, me, and all my friends took full advantage of it on the weekends. My house became the hangout for older teenagers, and we had plenty of "ragers". One particular night, A girl that came over had drunk so much beer that she started acting weird and passed out on the front lawn of my house. She was in some sort of coma and we panicked and argued over who was going to call the police. The groups of teenagers quickly vanished, everyone went back home, and we agreed to call the police from Megan's house since the party was at my house. Darla lay halfway between the 2 houses on the corner of Tareyton Drive below the stop sign.

The ambulance came, took her to the hospital where she was dying from alcohol poisoning. Thankfully she recovered quickly and we never talked again. Darla was older than me, and previously had spent lots of time together. She was the one that actually taught me how to shave my legs. My mom had never prepared me for any right of passage of being a young woman and so I had to figure all the crap out on my own. Darla was shaving her legs in the bedroom one night I had slept over at her house and I asked her to show me. Who shaves in the bedroom? What a weird experience.

Darla's mom called around to all her daughter's friends to try to find out who the culprit was. No one made her daughter drink, it was her own fault, but yes, it was my house that opened up a space for teenagers to conduct illegal activity and it didn't end with that bender either.

Megan was clearly the reason why I was being ridiculed at school, and it got so bad, that I constantly was seen crying at school until my Science teacher noticed. She was the only teacher up to that point that had ever acted as if she cared about the students...or at least showed kindness towards me. She called me into her office, and Jim was already there waiting for me. She had heard what kids were saying about us, and we quickly denied all claims, even though it was really the truth. I was a slut, and nothing less than that. I deserved to be called all those terrible things. I started dressing slutty as well, though it was the "style" too. Knee high stockings, half cut shirts with no bra.. I wasn't the only one who dressed like that. I knew it was bad when a male teacher came up to me after class and told me to "never wear that in my class again" I didn't understand why, but looking back I sure did. I remember that specific outfit well, I wore a skin tight top, jean shorts above the knee, and knee high black stockings that were being held up by a very visible garter belt. Talk about sex appeal. I had wondered why he kept looking at my legs in class, making me constantly cross my legs back and forth. What I was wearing made him physically uncomfortable and I just thought I was being "punk".

The Science teacher had said some really great stuff that helped me get over things. Her advice was to straight up ignore people when they said things. Do not give them any rope to hang myself with and eventually it would all go away. Or better yet, agree to it, laugh at yourself and it will go away quicker. That's what I did, and she was right. At that age it's really hard to see the bigger picture of life. All I wanted to do was die, die a horror death like Freddy Kruger slicing my throat with his sharp finger knives. But the nightmare was finally over and Jim and I's relationship only grew stronger after that. We knew the only people we could trust was each other.

My mom was more frequently getting DUIs, and the law wasn't as strict back then as it is now but with this one she was forced to do community service. Once a week I would have to take time away from my boyfriend to drive my mom to the fire station to perform her community service. Of course, she wasn't allowed to drive there because she had no license, and I was only like 14 so I had to go to the parking lot across the street, drop her off, drive down the street for a few hours until it was time to pick her back up again. We would drive to the bank parking lot where she then would get out of the passenger's side and cross the street to the fire station. This went on until she fulfilled her appointed hours of service to the community.

Things started getting really bad again at home as I constantly tested my mom's limits as she continued to push my buttons. She still thought she had power over me, even though I did whatever the hell I wanted, when I wanted. It grew increasingly strained as she searched for love and affection from all the wrong places herself.

Though I was the one parenting, it was increasingly more difficult to get her awake in the morning for work, and I had stopped caring whether or not she made it to work. She spent more and more time hungover during the week, and missed more and more work days. The tension got so bad, that it was just a matter of time before someone got hurt. I just never had enough guts to kill myself. Although I tried cutting my wrists, it is actually more difficult than you think. I guess I didn't really want to die that much.

One night I awoke to my mom screaming my name as she collapsed in the foyer onto the floor. She was wearing a white lace top, and some sort of short skirt, and there was blood dripping everywhere. I had no idea what to do as my mom lay dying in front of me. She slurred her words so badly that I could barely understand a single word that came out of her mouth. I pulled her up with all of my strength to lay her upright on the big circle "papasan" chair. By now I was already used to taking care of her, so this was no big deal to me. She often passed out at random times during the day or night, and I always put a pillow under her head, a blanket over her body, but more often than not, I would have to make sure she didn't burn the house down because 99 percent of the time there would be a lite cigarette in her hand. Usually draped over some sort of very flammable cloth, couch, fabric, carpet or even near a lighter...but hardly ever draped over an actual ashtray. I started trying to compete with each forgotten lite cigarette to see how long the ash could get before I could get to it. I often asked God to intervene and help me, but I always felt like I wasn't ever worthy of his love. I constantly felt bad for myself and wondered what life would be like if.....if things were different.

Seeing the blood drip down and on her white lace shirt, made me scared. I looked around and couldn't find the source of the blood until I looked at her wrists. She slit her wrists. I panicked and did something smart and called 911. I put bandages on her wrists and waited for the ambulance as I tried to comfort her by letting her know help was on the way. It must have sobered her at least half way up because she started screaming at me, without moving very much.

"We don't have insurance to pay for that. Who is going to pay for that? No, no, no, tell them to go away. Tell them to go away." I heard the ambulance coming down the stretch of road from the main street and ran outside to make sure they didn't step foot out of the ambulance.

"Please, we can't afford the ambulance. Please leave." I begged the EMT workers to leave.

I was desperate to help my mom, even though I hated her, I tried to sob at the technicians for sympathy, but they tried pleading with me to let them in the house. I told them we had no health insurance, and they understood and eventually turned around the cul de sac to venture back to wherever they came from. Problem averted. Money was more important than health in her world.

I didn't understand what my mom was going through, nor did I care. All I wanted was to feel loved, and apparently so did my own mother. She mumbled under her breath how no one loved her, how no one cared about her, as tears streamed down her face. I quickly countered her negative feelings with words of encouragement, as to how much I loved her and cared about her, though she fought real hard against them. I repeated it over and over again, as I went to get a blanket for her as she started to fall asleep. Draped into this odd shaped chair, with her hair and make up a mess, dried blood all over her clothes and fading fast to sleep. This was something that wasn't totally out of the ordinary.

I was really starting to have enough of all of this, and spent less and less time at home, as if that was even possible. But Jim's family really took me under their wings and I became a part of their family. I think my mom was really jealous because she tried to break us up. Of course that wasn't going to happen, and eventually she tried to be physical with me again so I ran away from home. I did this often for hours or days at a time, but this time was different. I reached my limit. After about a week, my mom ended up calling the police and made me out to be this terrible kid that ran away because I didn't like her "rules". She already knew where I was, so it was no surprise when the police showed up at Jim's parents house. They spoke to Jim's mom and knew I was being abused, and pleaded with the police, but it did no good. My mom and Jim's mom both met down at the station to discuss what was to become of me.

They eventually agreed to me staying with Jim's family for another week, then I would have to make my way back home.

After the time had lapsed and I had returned home the things were never talked about, or resolved. History sure does repeat itself. I realize where the problem started that I have been dealing with while I was married. Whenever my husband and I argued, I hated talking about it to the point where I ignored it and tried to just tell him to forget it. I liked to go to bed angry and wake up pretending it never happened. I had always been one who avoided confrontation at any cost. It was a pattern that was created and I have had to create a new pattern of facing the confrontation head on to resolve it.

I have often ignored things in my marriage that any normal person would have a serious problem with. This is obviously where it stemmed from. I never learned how to confront issues and resolve things, especially while in a relationship with another person whether it being a family member, friend or a boyfriend.

I had spent 2 weeks at my boyfriend's house, to which we had freedom to be intimate with each other in a sexual way whenever we wanted, and as teenagers did with raging hormones, it was often. I had found the love I was searching for and it wasn't from the unconditional love of a parent. It was from sex. I loved it, as did Jim, and I couldn't get enough of it.

Our relationship soon turned into just sex. Making sure we pleased each other of course, but there was not much else left. After 2 and a half years of being together, I yearned for more and more of it from other people. This was the start of me actually becoming the thing that other kids gossiped about. I was addicted to recieving love through sex, I became addicted to it.

The breakup with Jim was really hard. I tried and tried, but he was heartbroken. I did whatever I wanted to, I flirted with boys, made him jealous on purpose, and then when I wanted sex and had no one to have it with, he was the first person I would call, and he never said no to me. Ever.

Before we broke up Jim's parents started going through a divorce, and his dad ended up moving out and getting a house by himself to which we would go visit him now and then. Jim stayed in the big family house, until a later date to which his mom ended up moving into a brand new townhouse in another school district. The opposing district to our Neshaminy. I hated his new friends before he even made them. He made lots of new friends in his new fancy neighborhood, to which I quickly became jealous of all the beautiful girls that wanted to know the new Italian strapping handsome growing boy that just moved in. We both took turns making each other jealous which turned into a real toxic relationship in the end and we spent months doing this instead of just moving on.

At one point, I had stayed at my friend's house, Joelle, for days and days. She had an older brother who was really hot. He loved to walk around the house with no shirt on, and I drooled over his skinny, naturally tan body. I lay in bed with him, having snuck out of Joelle's room, over to him across the hall. I was in lust for him, and it was the only reason I could give to Jim to say that it was finally over.

I had called him from Joelles to break up with him and he lost it. Eventually, my mom came to pick me up from there having been roped in from Jim. My mom and Jim both pleaded with me to not let it end the whole ride home. It was awkward and all I wanted to do was to run away.

We went back to our house, where Jim and I talked for awhile, and of course ended up having sex. What else was there to do? It was an end to the awkward realization of leaving each other. We continued to just become house calls for each other, as we played the field never fully again committing to each other until he had a new girlfriend and I just went on being intimate with every boy who would look at me. It was my first ever real relationship, and I had learned from the best role model as to how a relationship was supposed to be like. I compared every man I had ever dated to Jim. I was also just starting the age of being able to work, so my world just became a whole lot bigger.

6

Coma

One night Kelly, Jim and I were deciding on what to do and we chose to go to a party at Jim's friend's house across town. My mom and her boyfriend were home, and had his crappy pick up truck, so I asked to borrow her car to go out. Despite Jim having a license, I decided to drive, even though I had no idea where it was.

We literally didn't even make it down to the first light when I went through a yellow light and watched it turn in the rear view mirror. No sooner did I look away, did I see red shining police lights all around me. I freaked out and turned down a side street and, not even paying attention, slammed the car into park while the car was still moving. We had a huge jerk movement before we came to a screeching halt. The policeman told me I had run a red light, which was a total lie. And when I told him I didn't have a license, he had a look on his face like he found gold. There goes our fun Saturday night. He called my mom and I was so scared as to what was going to happen. She was going to beat the crap out of me for sure. And in front of my friends. I just knew it.

Neither my mom, nor her boyfriend had a license either. So when I saw them driving up, I was really nervous of what might take place. They were smart, and pulled over on the other side of the street. Her boyfriend stayed in the car, as my mom came over, claimed responsibility for me, and ownership of the car. She drove us off in the back and nervously drove back to the house. My friends didn't get off without a hitch either, they took Kelly's information, but since she had no license, she was given a warning. Jim however, received a very large fine for letting me drive, while he remained in the passenger's side.

We walked into the house, and my mom and her boyfriend started dying laughing. Calling me a jailbird, and saying hahaha you got in trouble! Haha haha I was so relieved that I didn't get yelled at. The next day, my mom took me to court and paid all the fines. The court did tell me that I would have a serious problem when I did become of age to go get my license. It made me scared to go get it, but I failed the test twice and eventually moved to the city, where I rode my bike everywhere. I didn't end up getting a license till I was in my mid 20's and only because I was pregnant. I never did have a problem or a "mark" on my record of the incident.

So by now Simpson, my mom's boyfriend, has become a regular occurrence in our lives. He spent time at our house, we spent time at his, and it was a different sort of relationship from the beginning. Another biker gang member, Simpson, was actually very different from the rest. He still drank and smoked a lot, but didn't seem to have the same sort of "douchebag" attitude that my mom seemed to go for. I am sure, they were not without their arguments, but he really made my mom a different person.

My mother had already been in the hospital at least 24 hours before Simpson had taken us to go see her. I remember him calling us on the phone to tell us what happened, and I just sat there frozen with the receiver in my hand with the long phone cord attached to the phone hanging on the wall in the kitchen. I wasn't upset then, and I wasn't upset now. I just didn't care plus she wanted to die, so let her get what she wanted. My grandparents were there, and everyone just stared at her while she lay there in silence. I just couldn't muster up enough emotions to even fake a tear. Each day went by, and we just waited to see what was going to happen. So do we wait it out, or do they pull the plug, eventually? Please let it be over soon, I kept thinking to myself.

Three long days later, we got a call. She is out of the coma. Simpson comes by to pick us up, and we go over there where my Gramma is already waiting by her side. I remember my Gramma pleading and pleading with her to not do this again.

You have to stop drinking.

Please, what are you doing with your life?

You are so lucky.

You shouldn't be living like this.

My mom, shaking her head, has no memory at all of the entire situation. Which wasn't the first time, and certainly not the last time of her blackouts. Not to be confused with the black outs from rehab. An alcohol induced blackout is when you drink so much, your brain stops thinking. That's not the definition of the black out, but you get the idea. I know, because I had a few myself. Once I was drinking with a bunch of older teenagers, and drank so much that I didn't know how I had gotten home, let alone what I did that night. Your body still acts, your brain still responds and acts like you're drunk but you have no memory of it at all, and you are basically lost in time and space. The other time I blacked out was during my college years.

My mother agreed to everything my Gramma said. Over and over again. Promises that were only meant to be broken. I really wasn't all that happy she had made it out alive. I knew in my heart that it didn't matter what had happened to her, she would go back to drinking and being a part of the bar hopping lifestyle.

We ended up having to stay with my Gramma for a few days, until the hospital decided that my mom had to stay under "observation" while they evaluated her so a team of professionals could decide if they could risk letting her out back into society.

The smart professionals decided after a week that she was incapable of taking care of herself, or staying sober, and forced her into an in patient treatment.

She spent 3 months mandatory time in a facility. We were forced to live with my Grandfather and his second wife. Though they lived only a few streets over from our townhouse development, in a nice upscale house on a wealthy street, we barely ever saw him. Him and his second wife, or sometimes even the mistress, would often be seen walking around the park in front of our house. They never stopped by to check in, they never came over for dinner, they never asked if we needed help, or how our lives were. We saw him on Christmas, and Easter. If you wanted your check, you had to go visit him. $100 each visit. He wouldn't even make out the check to you unless you came to his house. The card, and checks would always be sitting on the kitchen table, and it wasn't until he was satisfied with your company, did he remove himself from the living room, make his way down the kitchen table to neatly write out your check, your card and then hand it to you.

My mom made me terrified of this man. So scared of him, and everything he did. Make sure you put your knife on the plate with the serrated edge facing inward, at a perfect angle, so as to not fall onto the table. Make sure you do what he says, listen to him talk, and never talk back. I was told he was an evil, terrible man and that he didn't like me. I was forced to see him so my mom could get her checks. All she seemed to care about was money. It has been a trend that has still continued to this day.

While my mom was away at the inpatient rehabilitation facility, I wandered around the neighborhoods, trying to find things to do. Often walking along the train tracks behind my Grandfather's house, rolling down the hills, placing rocks or other found objects along the tracks to see if we could hear them when a train came passing by. There was a creek, with a rope swing, trails to explore, boys to find. I ended up meeting the older neighbor teenager that lived a few houses down. Steve was his name and he drove an IRoc Z28. Having a rich family usually meant once you had a license, you had a car. He quickly found an interest in me, and so we hung out a lot that summer. Usually our favorite thing to do was to hide out in the shed in his backyard and just make out. He was cute for sure, but I suspect that maybe he was a bit of the nerdy type that tried real hard to be cool. I was his way of being able to learn how to be with girls, in a non threatening way. It was fine with me of course, but his braces were really annoying. By this point, it was clear to me that I was following in my mother's footsteps and I just didn't care about it. After all, it made me feel better, even if it was only temporary. It was attention that wasn't painful.

Simpson took us to visit my mom once a week, and that was indeed painful. I didn't want to go at all. I had no desire to see her, or to be fake and pretend that I wanted to. One of the qualities I did end up having was never being able to be fake. I don't know where it came from, but I can tell when a person is being fake and ingenuine right away and I can't stand it. Luckily now it's not in my life anymore.

We had no relationship, and the fact that she wasn't drunk meant that neither of us knew how to act around the other. It was downright painful to be there, though she must have loved to have visitors. After all, you make "friends" on the inside, as I also ended up experiencing being in an inpatient facility. You talk about your families, your jobs, your life away from this sober house, and then you get to show off once your visitors arrive. "See, here's my wonderful daughter, isn't she great?" In reality she hated me with every ounce of her being. The feelings were mutual.

There was this big room where we would have to visit with her in. It was like a mess hall, a slash game room. It had tables, chairs and board games that children of this current generation think are extinct. Personally, I always loved playing board games. My sister and I never got along growing up, and always argued about who was winning or cheating and so it never went anywhere. For the record, I never cheated at games, I didn't see the point.

We usually opted for Scrabble when visiting my mom, or just smoking cigarettes. She would remove herself, go smoke outside and 15min later reappear as if it didn't disrupt anything. I didn't care. I didn't want to be there either.

After 3 months, she was released back home, and I was finally allowed to enter back into my house as well. It was very quiet and uneventful living with my grandfather, but I really had no problems with it except that I could tell at that point that he really did seem to hold a grudge against me, being his daughter's daughter. The daughter that made an embarrassment out of him. Him, who was an actual doctor, who had gotten a ton of respect and was an active member of the community. He owned the largest and most successful veterinary clinic within the county. He had donated tons of money and time to local organizations yet he never once came to visit his own grandchildren. When my grandfather had died when I was an adult, I had learned just how mad he was at my mother. It was time for them to read his will, and it still included every alteration he had made to it through the lawyers. During the time of this happening he had cut her out of his will completely, as well as my sister and I, innocent bystanders to her poor decisions in life. Don't worry, she got some of his money in the end. That's all she was waiting for anyway. He did end up changing it back before he had actually passed. But the damage was done as we all got to witness the crossing out and then adjustment later to her portion of the estate.

It's ok, I didn't know any better at that age so it didn't really affect me. I was just glad to get out of his house, where I had rules. I wish I could tell you that was the end to the story for the most part, but it's not.

Three months away wasn't long enough for my mother. She did try though. She lasted a few weeks, trying to stay away from the *people, places, things* which in addict terms refers to all the triggers that keep us from our sobriety and cause you to relapse.

You are supposed to stay away from the people that you do the drugs/drinking with. Social demands I think are really the main reason for a lot of drug problems in the beginning, especially when you're young. Everyone wants friends, and no one wants to be made fun of. "Things" refer to the things that are associated with the use. And Places, obviously, are the places you would go to use. Be it the bar, a certain friend's house, or maybe even the state park, which is what another boyfriend I had named Jim and I used to do in order to smoke pot or take acid.

Why go to the bar if you're not going to drink? The cravings are just too much when you're just out of recovery. Sometimes we may think we are strong, but you get there and it's just too much to resist. "It's just one drink" said every alcoholic at one point in their life. I know from experience, that it never stays at one if you haven't gotten to the root of the problem that created the addiction in the first place.

She tried to stay away from her biker friends, from her biker boyfriend, from the bars, from the drinking. But it didn't last. She didn't want to quit, and that's the main problem with trying to stay sober. You have to want to change, and she just didn't want to change. She tried to hide it, she put up a good front for a week or two, she just couldn't stand being at home. When you look in the mirror and don't like what you see, you turn a blind eye to it. Simpson came back around and then she was roped back into the bar scene. I'm not blaming it on him, of course. Having things go back to normal actually felt comfortable again. Despite it being a living hell, it's all I knew. I knew what to expect, and I knew how to take care of myself. I knew how to survive it.

7

Suffer

It became a habit of sneaking out of my second floor bedroom window. I would lock my bedroom door, climb out the window, down the shed, grab the metal rain gutter and slowly lower one foot onto the fence, and then the other foot until I was just balanced enough to bring both hands down and jump off. I would go out the back gate and just walk around town. Sometimes meeting up with random boys, or friends, or just walking to the store and then eventually making my way back home to sneak in the front door. The front door always made a noise when you opened it, and it was right below my mother's bedroom so I always tried extra carefully not to make a peep. Which I think about now and think how ridiculous it was because my mom slept like a rock from the moment she closed her eyes. Her sleeping pills were alcohol, and so when she passed out, there was NO WAY to wake her up. Nevertheless, I still went about going through the motions. I never really did anything fantastic on my excursions late at night, but it still felt like I was the one in control. That's what the constant tension was between my mother and I. Control. Who had control over the other. Another aha moment. Yet another reflection of problems in my marriage to this day. Though through the act of practicing yoga, I have been able to let go of almost all of my control.

Control. From the time I started venturing off to the city on the train, I was always the one to be in control. I was the only one of our friends who could read the map and figure out the train return and pick up times. I knew my way around the city and everyone left me in charge.

I would be the sober one at the Raves, I would be the one to get us all back together safe and sound, even if one of them was puking all night from ecstacy. I always felt in charge and like I had control. I was the one who rented the apartments and collected rent and bill money from all my roommates. I was the one who had to kick people out who refused to pay me the months of bills they owed me. I was always in control. Once my husband and I started dating it was so obvious that we were both in constant need of trying to control each other. He had the exact opposite kind of childhood that I had however, he was not without his own kind of trauma experience.

My new found skills of sneaking out, and skipping school, only fueled my act of rebellion. I didn't give a crap about anything, and it's amazing that nothing actually really serious happened to me..Oh wait. How quickly I forget.

With my new found freedom, I got my first job at Drug Emporium, courtesy of a friend named Jane. She often would pick me up and drop me off, or I would beg my mom to drop me off, and have to fend for herself to get rides home after work. Often ending at 9:30 at night, it was a hard sell, especially on a school night. I didn't care though, and taking working very seriously and walking was always an option. Drug Emporium was way behind in technology and still had yet to install a scanning system. Can you imagine, I had to type in every SKU number for every product bought. A combination of like 12 or so numbers, and I had to enter every single number, and then add the sale price number. It was ridiculous. So the next time you get impatient while waiting in line to purchase something, have a little heart for those of us who had to slave over tiny little digits for hours at a time for a measly $4.25 an hour. And no, I didn't work to spend money. It was the only way I was able to survive. I worked to put food in my mouth, I worked to buy my own clothes, or bus/ train transportation or what later became, cigarette and drug money. I mean you know it was only a matter of time before that started to happen.

This was about the time when I walked into school, just like any other, the previous few days were the same as any other. Nothing out of the "ordinary" which obviously meant, taking care of myself, doing my homework, making dinner, or what I could scrape together. Just living..day to day. I was walking down the hall making my way to my locker when a kid I knew walked up to me and asked in a real sarcastic sort of way "Hey Jen, can I get some drugs off your mom?" and then chuckled. I asked what on earth he was talking about, and he repeated himself, although this time he actually seemed to be a little bit more serious. I had no idea what he was talking about, of course, and just gave him a dirty look as I started to walk away. Of course, gossip spreads like wildfire, especially back then, as we had no cell phone or Youtube videos for distractions. It came back around to me, and apparently his mom had read it in the newspaper that my mom got arrested, with a male in the passenger's side for drunk driving. As they proceeded to search the car, they found drugs. At this point in time, I have no recollection as to what they were, but I remember the article using the term that classified a whole array of drugs, such as "Opiates" or "Barbiturates" or something to that effect. Of course, we had had health class years earlier where we learned all that useless information. but when you're actually experiencing these things you don't know or care what the correct classification is for it. Soon everyone started asking to buy drugs off me. I honestly don't know if they were serious, or if they in fact would have bought it off me. By the time I got home that day from school everyone had heard about it.

My mom was fired or had quit her great job right after that had happened. Things became more unstable. I became an expert as to how many beers she had. I could tell if it was a new buzz- an old buzz, a fast buzz, or an all day buzz. It was usually a 24 hour buzz, as the moment she woke up in the mornings she usually had another beer for breakfast..or on special occasions. a bloody mary with lots of cracked pepper. She loved Bloody Marys.

I honestly don't know how she survived with no income. On top of it she was also on house arrest at some point as well. I can't remember the amount of time she was on house arrest for but I will never forget her having to measure how far out the door she could reach before the ankle bracelet started beeping or instigate the phone calls. The phone call of the automated service to make sure that you were indeed in the house and sober at the time of the call. She had to speak into the phone and had to pick it up after a certain amount of rings or it would render her awol.

Either way, the punishments would end but she would resume her career which she always was very good at, spending time and money at the local bars. Maybe she used her good looks for men to buy her drinks. I know she occasionally brought some of these men home before Simpson. They would do the walk of shame down the stairs, and I would catch a glimpse of them leaving out the door, as the man (insert name here) would either go back to his place or get dropped off somewhere. There were a few of them that stuck around a little longer, of course it never ended well for them. One in particular was a real douche bag. All her boyfriends were in the biker scene. They all had reputations that you didn't want to mess with. I heard many stories of them talking about killing people, but most of the stories were of beating the crap out of people, or damaging property, or stealing stuff. Nothing ever phased me, as I was always around people like this. But this dude...huge guy with dark hair. Derek. He stuck around for a while, and treated my mom and I like total garbage. He expected to be waited on, hand and foot, as if he were a king, and our home his castle. He would make lewd comments to me, as if it were OK that he made sexual comments to the daughter of the lady he was screwing. He wasn't the only one. But part of me wonders if the things they said were actually inappropriate, or if it was just because of my trauma history. I will never know the truth because I was so blinded by the trauma. There was one guy though..big, hairy biker. Always made comments to me, and I always had this "feeling" around him. It was a feeling that had I been home alone, or in the dark, I would have no chance in hell of wrestling him off of me. There are people that give off the creepy vibe, and he was the definition of creepy. I wouldn't be surprised if he was a predator who had to register whenever he moved. They would always comment on how beautiful I was, just like my mother. But the energy behind it always felt disgusting in my body.

Derek was less creepy, but just as much as an asshole as the rest of the douchebags my mom associated with. Always men. I had only ever met one woman my mom hung out with, Mia, who was part Native American, had long dark hair and who wore braids. I remember her because she ended up living on our couch for months. That was nothing odd at our house either. Random dudes sleeping in my bed..yes, MY bed. After a late night of partying, maybe the parties came back to our house, one lucky guy would get my moms bed, the 3rd wheel would get the couch sometimes, but 9 times outta 10 times they chose my bed to crash in. I would be coming home from sleepovers or coming back from partying myself from the city, and the worst feeling would hit me when I would open my door to see that I wouldn't be able to crash in my own bed. It felt so violating. I would have to sleep on the second couch, or on the floor somewhere.

Mia was a little different. She slept on the couch for like a month, and let me drive her car to school. I would pick up a few friends beforehand, and we would roll up and park acting real cool cause I had a car. It wasn't anything remotely cool and the brakes were so bad that I had to pump them like crazy a mile up the road so I did not cause an accident. One day I must have been ½ inch away from the bumper in front of me while trying to break going down a hill. I thought for sure it was going to be the end of my illegal driving career. Luckily, I survived those drives. Anyway, Mia actually asked me how my day was, and acted as if she cared. The sad part was that as soon as I started to really get to know her, and love her, she vanished. One day I woke up and she was gone, and I never saw her again.

Derek was in and out but there was one incident that apparently was just too much for my mom to deal with and he finally stopped coming around. My friends and I were hanging out in my house, and my Mom and Derek arrived, and kicked us all out. They immediately started arguing while we were still inside the house as my friends and I started to leave and walk out the door. When it got really heated and loud, I ran back inside only to see him throwing my mom all over the house like a ragdoll. I thought I was tough, so I tried fighting him as he just laughed in my face. I yelled for my friends to come inside and help, as if that was going to do anything.

My mom just stood there crying as he wound up his arm behind him and let his fist loose on my mom's face. The swing was so hard that she flew into the air and landed on this square glass table that was a few feet behind her in the middle of the living room, shattering it into a thousand pieces. That was the point I called the police as my friends ran back out the door, scared out of their minds. The police came and rolled their eyes as they entered the house. They knew us all by name by that point. It was almost a huge joke to them. The neighbors would call the police on us, either for my parties, or for me screaming bloody murder while being abused, whether it was me calling because my mom slit her wrists, or her when she went into cardiac arrest from a bee sting, arguments with boyfriends, vandalized cars, breaking into the front window because I lost my key, calling the police because my mom broke my bedroom window throwing rocks at it cause she was drunk and couldn't get in, or if it was because some jerk just broke my mom's nose.....we were very, very well known at that residancece. All that stuff was happening, and still no one questioned my mother's parenting skills.

Derek was the guy that got arrested with my mom during the traffic stop. She pinned all the stuff on him, so of course we all believed her. I wanted to believe her.

After he left, some other guy took his spot. Some short guy who ended up living with us for a while. It wasn't ever a celebration, it would be one day I walk in the house, and there would be some random guy there. Using the kitchen, eating our food, what little food we had, sleeping in my mom's bed. I never had conversations with these men. It was a mutual respect that we just never crossed. I'll pretend you are not here, and you do the same and we will live in this house peacefully. Until one day he accused me of stealing his brick of weed that he had in the nightstand on his side of my mothers bed. Don't get me wrong, I often went through my mom's stuff. Mostly to look at pictures, and to catch a glimpse as to what it was like to be an adult. When there were men living with us, I stayed away. I learned my lesson on numerous occasions. I had seen things that I wish I could UNSEE. Images burned in my mind that have forever haunted me. Why the locks on the door were never used is beyond me.

You see, we were 3 girls living together. My mom, my sister and I. We never had any healthy boundaries with each other. Something I have had to work very hard at later on in life.

One fine day, I went to see if my mom was awake and dressed as I had heard the shower running earlier. It was midday, and I still had not seen her leave the bedroom. Usually the protocol was to look outside and see if there was an extra car in the driveway. If there was, then you knew to stay away. If it was empty, then chances were, it was free to walk around our house in Pjs and no bra.

That day there was no car, because the loser didn't own one. I knocked as I started turning the doorknob. There was no noise as I walked in. I saw things I wish I hadn't and I immediately ran out of the room as my mom started laughing. I slammed my door so loud, and just started balling my eyes out. I was even more upset that she didn't even care that I had witnessed such a heinous event for a daughter to see. I wonder if it would have been different if he were my father. But these were always acts done with random men.

Needless to say, I knew to take precautions while there was a man living with us. This was no exception. I stayed away, and I wasn't the one to steal the brick of weed from my mom's boyfriend. In fact, stealing things was also another thing I became a victim of, and not just from my immediate family. That's for a different book though. So is the compulsive lying that I was victim to.

After the stunt with my mom being arrested for drugs, it just so happened that the police were on the "JUST SAY NO" campaign and during class one day I was called down to the social worker's office. I was brought into a room with 2 officers and a few other "troubled" kids. The police questioned us about where to get drugs, if we did drugs, and all sorts of dumb questions that I didn't want to be apart of. I, just like my mother, hated cops. Not because they were evil or because "F*ck the police" was a cool song, but because they had chances to help me several times, and never did anything about it. My dad eventually started to suspect my mom of shady things and would always order us to see counselors when he was in the states to do something about it. I was always either too scared to say anything, having been coached the entire drive to the court appointed therapy session, or the one or 2 times I did say something, they would bring my mom in right after who would say I was lying to seek attention. Nothing was ever done about anything. Don't get me wrong, times were a lot different back then. It was normal to hit your child for punishment. That whole generation was raised on getting a "whopping" or a belt to the butt. But this was different. Not saying any abuse is worse than another.

But the cops were pissing me off, and I started acting up, saying all kinds of things that I probably should have kept as secrets. Either way, I eventually found myself with CPS (Child Protective Services) coming to our house. My mother later said that she thinks she knows who called on us. Either way it didn't matter how they came to our family, they had to come to check to make sure we had food, to make sure we weren't being abused, or doing drugs, etc. My mom was tipped off of course, we all knew they were going to show up, so you know our cupboards were full of food that day. Didn't last long though because I was so used to not having food, once she did end up bringing food home, I would gorge myself with all of it until my stomach hurt. I just never knew when we would have food again, or maybe because I just wanted to feel a connection to something and food was the closest thing.

Our social worker was named Lucia, a pretty, young hispanic woman. She was nice, but you could tell she oozed with inexperience. So our family started playing this "game" with the government services. She would ask us questions, each individually and then as a group. They would be the same questions, and then she would compare them later to see if things added up. I would go on and on about the abuse, but the mental abuse never ended, nor did the neglect. I told the social worker the truth, as I had told councilors and therapists growing up. No one believed me. They just didn't want to or they were just convinced by my mom that I was telling a lie to get attention.

I would go into details about the week, as she would come once a week at a preset time. My mom did this, did that, blah blah. It didn't matter what I said, because the next thing the social worker would do is bring my mom in to sit on the other side of me and repeat everything I had just said. As my mom was a master manipulator, she always got Lucia on her side. We all just went through the motions, for every week we had to endure this ridiculous interrogation. The boyfriend I had at the time was even starting to attend the meetings as we both found them hysterical. He would sit next to me as I explained what was really happening and then he would witness as my mom would deny, deny, deny.

It was almost Christmas break in 10th grade at age 15, I had another few days of school left, as I made my way to my favorite class, Art. Just starting to get ready to finish a painting when someone walks in from the office, who proceeds to ask me to step out of the room, and gather my belongings.

I walk out of the Art room to see Lucia waiting for me, and directing me to take them to my locker. Totally unaware what was happening, I started walking to it, and looked at her, as she wouldn't look me in the eyes, and ignored all my questions.

I was defeated. She drove me straight to a rehab facility and I got locked up in a place for doing drugs when I wasn't even doing them. And to make matters worse, by the time I was out of "Black out" I tried calling my mom. No answer. I tried calling the social worker. Both of them were on vacation. My mom went to Mexico and Lucia was not in the office. Go figure, it was Christmas, and I was left there to be forgotten about until it was convenient for their schedules.

This wasn't the first time my mom went on vacation with a guy I had never met. Years earlier, we took a trip to Florida, to go to Disney World. I could not have been more happy, as a life of being in poverty, I never thought we would do anything fun or entertaining. I wish I knew how it went about happening, because once we got there, we weren't alone. I often wonder if this guy paid for the trip or if there was some other way we ended up there because it wasn't like my mom to take us places or do things with us that didn't benefit her. In the evening while at the hotel, a guy showed up at our room. That night, and every night after, the mysterious man lay in bed with my mother, having loud sex with her as I lay in the other double bed right next to them. I pretended to sleep the first night, but by the next night, I had enough. I wasn't able to get any sleep. I constantly interrupted them, asking for them to stop making so much noise, or to beg for them to stop. They replied with "Knock it off" and "Shut the f*ck up." I honestly don't remember even doing anything at Disney except eating at a Disney themed restaurant. I don't know if we even made it into the actual park. One of the things I noticed over time was that I seemed to remember only the terrible events of my life and not so much the beneficial ones, or the ones that tend to put a smile upon my face. It was either because there were not many of them to begin with or the amount of the terrible ones sure outweighed and drowned out all the tiny, happy ones. One of the days I spent the whole day in the pool at the hotel meeting a girl and playing pretend the whole day with her, with my mother nowhere to be found. So that's that.

This time, instead of bringing me along on her vacation, she decided to have me committed to an institution by lying to a government appointed CPS worker that I had a drug problem. That's a good babysitter.

I was there for a little over 2 weeks, as people started coming back from their Christmas and New years breaks, I finally started getting phone calls. My Dad called, and flew around the world to try to get me taken out, for which he was unsuccessful because he had no custody of us. His hands were tied behind his back. I did tell him the truth of what happened, and could tell he was heart broken. A few days later, my mom shows up with Christmas presents. 2 wrapped presents. One was a box of underwear. The other was a box of paper and envelopes. Talk about adding insult to injury. Here's some underwear because you're not coming home anytime soon. Write me some letters because I'm not calling you either.

Rehab wasn't all that terrible. We got to go out for a privilege, and we went bowling and to an ice cream shop. We pretended as though we were all in one misfit family for a day. All getting along, and pretending that we weren't calculating our escape plans. One of the boys did end up running, only later when we were back at the facility though. He ended up relapsing and found his way back within a few days. One of the reasons they try shipping you off to another county is for that exact reason. People, Places, Things. I sure learned a lot from going to rehab. The biggest lesson I learned was actually how to become a really good drug addict.

That's right, after being there for a few weeks, I had heard many telling stories about drugs. They sounded like something I really needed in my life, and I couldn't wait to get out to test them all out. Were these kids all telling me the truth? Were they that amazing and cool to do? I was dying to get out just to try it all. Eventually my mom came to pick me up, and rehab was never spoken about since, to this day actually. I never saw the social worker again either.

As soon as I got home, I went straight to the druggies at school. "Let's get high, I want in." And so went the downfall into more sex, drugs, alcohol and all other things that forgotten unloved kids do with free time, and not a care in the world.

Eventually, I had a new "serious" boyfriend, again, named Jim, an-other Jim. Again, he was much older than I, took me under his wings and taught me the way of the hippie lifestyle. Which meant, drinking, smoking cigarettes, lots of them, and weed. Lots of weed. I tried it all with him, but cigarettes were the only thing that really stuck on me, at least at that point in time anyway. I was 15 years old, and addicted to smoking. It was no problem for me. I had my own money now, and the freedom to buy cigarettes at the store, or the gas station down the road owned by foreigners who thought the law didn't apply to them. Maybe it did, maybe it didn't. But one day I went to the gas station while tripping on acid and attempted to buy a pack of "Jacks'" though not my brand. It was the only thing I could afford at the time, which was only 99 cents, and I tried to pay with all nickels. It did work in the end, but I had to convince him I was indeed old enough to buy cigarettes. I tried sticking to vending machines, yes they used to sell cigarettes out of vending machines! But my brand was often one of the first to be sold out. Newports, menthols. The worst of the worst. Smoking was hard to hide, but not really necessary. I mean I think the statistics of kids smok-ing if their parents smoked was like 9 to 1. I already grew up being made fun of for smelling like smoke, since second hand smoke wasn't even a thing yet. My hair was always ratty, and unkempt, my clothes were gross, I was white trash when I was little, and now I was just growing into to stereotype. It was a comfortable stereotype for me, I fit it to a T. Single parent household, mother with no money, a sibling, not being able to read or write very good, and now I smelled like smoke. I started smoking and I loved having sex and doing drugs and drinking beer. The love affair with Jim was solely based on being codependent. Don't get me wrong, we did have sex, but the more drugs he did, the less sex was had. He wanted it, but we ended up basically just making out. He was sweet and loving, and we cared about each other, but it wasn't very deep rooted. It wasn't intense like the love I had with Jim. It was an older mature love that was more internal than external. Maybe that's just the drugs talk-ing though. We spent most of our time eating at diners, driving around while smoking weed, or just parking and staring up at the sky. I honestly don't remember much of that year and half we spent together. He did help me keep my job by picking me up and dropping me off but I really think I did more harm to him then good. I think I was an escape for him as well. A way to get away from his own family life that was unpleasant to be around.

I was doing much better in school, and by now I had made an advancement to AP courses. But the pressures of having such an unbalanced home life made it impossible for me to keep my academics up. The English classes were especially hard for me. Reading assignments of like 5 chapters a night were just totally impossible for me. I faked it til I made it, which got me by for a while, but when we had pop up quizzes, I was quickly outed and eventually gave up and started failing on purpose. I asked my advisor at school if I could transition back to easier classes and she said that I couldn't go backwards unless I was failing. Failing on purpose seemed like the only viable option. I gave up on all home fronts, and half way through the school year, I went to the easy math class which was composed of all grades and ages from high school. I loved it, because it was practical math, for which you would actually need to use when you became an adult. For instance, we had to write out a check. That was easy for me, I had already been writing checks, paying bills, buying groceries, making spreadsheets for the money I had been making for a few years by the time I made it to that class. The class consisted of mostly 11th and 12th graders who couldn't maintain grades in classes at their own level, and then there was me, the 10th grader. I wore my maroon colored JNCo jeans and oversized skateboarding brand t-shirt, and quickly found a fit amongst the other outsiders. The sweet, blonde girl next to me couldn't for the life of her, figure out how to write a check. I took it upon myself to help her out, and she became my instant best friend. We had similar styles, loved the same type of music, and both had annoying little sisters to bond over. I loved Kelly, and still have a friendship with her to this day. She's probably one of the only people that would still help me out or be there for me, no matter what.

Kelly was and is a great friend. We hung out all the time. We were inseparable. But I am afraid I may have really gotten her started on the wrong path with my drug induced lifestyle.

I spent most of my time with Jim, for a while until shortly after I had contracted an STD. Not from him. I had actually gotten it not from sex, but by sharing clothes with another girl who had it. It was pubic lice, crabs. It was one of the most terrible things I had ever had the chance to endure physically. I couldn't go to my mom about it, because then she would think I'm having sex, obviously, but that wasn't a conversation I wanted to have. I didn't know I had it for a while until I just couldn't stop itching. It got worse and worse, until I realized what it was. I was petrified, mortified. Insert any word here, and that's how I felt. I spent hours at school, unable to sit still because it was so uncomfortable and hurt so much. They multiplied like crazy until I could see what looked like my whole private area moving. Clear colored and small, these little bugs hurt like hell. It was living torture and it had no end in site.

I did everything I could to try to get rid of them on my own. Of course, pre google days, it was hard. I wasn't about to go to the library and look up STDs as a teenager in a small neighborhood. I ended up finding that taking long hot baths usually helped a lot, and of course I shaved every pubic hair I could find. I would sit over the toilet for hours after school just plucking away at them. The amount reduced dramatically and I thought I had a hold of it, but as a teenager, I wasn't exactly concerned as much as I should have been about my cleanliness. Which is what got me in that situation in the first place. Borrowing clothes from numerous friends and family without washing them, was just a way of life. I guess that's why I have such a problem with being such a neat freak now. Though having kids certainly changed that recently, I used to spend 3 days a week just cleaning my house. It could never be clean enough for me. Trauma will do that to people.

I thought I was almost out of the woods when my boyfriend Jim started itching. I was mortified. We hadn't been having sex, but I guess it just was eventually going to happen. Laying on top of each other, sleeping next to each other on the couch. It was just a simple transfer. He on the other hand couldn't take it, and immediately went to the doctors which gave him a shampoo, like a lice sort of shampoo and it was gone in an instant. I used the rest of what he had, and thank god the horror was over. Needless to say, that pretty much ended our relationship. He really thought I had cheated on him, since it was an STD, but I didn't. Just wrong pants, wrong time.

8

Shudder To Think

The pressures of school and friends once in higher grades never really affected me as much as it did in elementary and jr high. In fact I had grown to have a really cool reputation because everyone knew my mom didn't care about anything I did. Parties every weekend while she was away, beer, cigarettes, condoms, a party all of the time.

Kids would have sex or make out all over my house. One time a couple had sex on my bed, and the guy threw the used condom out on my window sill. That was a cleanup I didn't really want to have to do myself. It was always a little chaotic having people over. I would tell them to be quiet outside, trying to make sure people smoked out back, even though my mom smoked so much, she would have never known. I guess I was just always concerned with someone lighting something on fire. Cleaning up was always annoying because drunk teenagers don't really tend to be neat. One time someone dropped my mom's vinegar dressing bottle all over the carpet and I just couldn't clean it up no matter how hard I tried. I had to improvise and decided that the living room just needed a makeover, and so I rearranged the furniture so the huge discolored carpet was not sitting directly under an oversized blue armchair. My mom came home and was really impressed and so it stayed for a long time. Not that she had any sense of styling a house. At one point we had 3 TVs...all one on top of the next. The big TV stopped working, so she trash picked another one which was then placed on top, and then another. Each TV being smaller than the previous. By the time I moved out of that townhouse, we had like 6 lawnmowers which in itself made no sense since nobody living in the house ever mowed the lawn, nor would it have mattered because none of them even worked. My step grandfather came over every week and mowed in the summer. He would pull up on the side of the house since we lived on the corner lot, pull off the mower, mow the lawn, and then leave. Again, another person in my life that never thought to communicate with me, or had anything to say to any of us living in that house in Langhorne PA. Somehow things just started to accumulate in that house. More and more objects started showing up, and nothing of any importance. My mom started to have a bit of a hoarding problem, which I later saw in other family members as well.

The parties were fun, but what made it more fun was my new friend Anne. She became like my pet when we were drinking. My little pet drunk that I turned into a lesbian. Get a few drinks in her, and she would make out with me all night long. I know it's not because she was attracted to women. I would have gladly made out with her day/ night drunk/high, sober. No, she wasn't attracted to me. She was a prude, virgin in high school with so much sexuality she just didn't know what to do with it. She loved how it turned all the guys on, as they would crowd around us while I straddle her on the carpet floor in the dining room. We would make out for what seemed like ever. We had nowhere to be, I had no parents, and no rules. I could do anything I wanted. This drug induced love affair went on for a long time. I would often tease her about it when we were sober, and it was as if she was pretending she were two different people. It was fine with me though. As long as she still drank, a lesbian love affair was always on the table.

Anne was a great friend to me for a while until she started hanging out with my sister and then all we did was fight over who was going to hang out with who. This was a theme of my entire childhood growing up. The same thing happened with Megan across the street and numerous other friends.

It was that time of year again when people went on vacations, my mom and Simpson were no exception. My friend Kelly that I met in

Math class had a younger sister who was the same age as my sister, and her family and her were all going on a trip to the Jersey shore. Kelly asked me to go months earlier, and of course I was dead set on going. My mom started planning her vacation, without us of course, and wanted to make sure we had somewhere else to go so we couldn't have any parties while she was away. Well a few days before the vacation my sister tells my mom that she's also going on the vacation with Kelly and her family. I was so pissed because I really didn't want to be around her, and of course, I confronted Kelly about it. I had assumed that my sister was going to be a tag along with Kelly's sister, but when Kelly told me that she had invited her, I was floored because she was only allowed to bring one friend. I was in panic mode because I didn't want to spend 4 days with either of my grandparents. Kelly begged her mom, but since her sister was bringing another friend, there were just too many kids, and the answer was no. Kelly said that my sister and I had to figure out who was going to go to the shore because she didn't want to have to pick. Teenage logic, go figure.

I caved in, as I always have done in the past, and just said my sister can go. I'll figure out something else. Turns out Kelly's sister's friend had an older sister, who lived on the finished basement floor of their large house and they had said I could crash there until my mom came back home. I would be out of sight, and no one would even know I was there.

I agreed, and so it was a plan. I arrived at this family home, and was escorted into the basement of this college girls wing of the house. Everything was painted blue, with hand painted dolphins on the wall. Her bedroom was a scene straight from the beach. Her name was Jane, of course, and she was in fact a full fledged lesbian. She was a small petite woman with really short butchy hair, and she always wore a hat or a bandana to cover it. No makeup, and very boyish types of clothes. The first night, I slept down there, with no bother from anyone and she brought me some food and left me alone.

The next morning, she had asked if I wanted to do something out of the house, and of course I agreed. She had this crappy 90's jeep, with no windows or top on it, and with no plan as to what to do, we just hit the highway. We were going north on 95 with no destination in mind, and no limit to what fun we could have. We talked for a while, but mostly just stared out into the landscaping while the wind whipped my hair around.

Each sign that went by, we would talk about the name of the town, or city and say, would that be a good place to pull over at? Shall we explore that place? We didn't stop until we ended up in Boston, Mass. Still not sure where to go, we drove around a little bit through the city until we ended up at a pier that seemed like the cool, hip place to be on a weekend. Beautiful weather outside, we followed large groups of people to the pier where there were boats all around us, with water and lots of food vendors. We ended up directly in the middle of some sort of food festival. If memory serves me, it was corn or chowder, or some crap like that. We ate and walked around until the sun started to go down, and we made it back to her jeep, and headed home..rather back to her beachy bedroom.

The next day she had already had plans to meet her friends at LBI (Long Beach Island) and asked if I wanted to tag along. Of course I said yes, especially since the previous day had turned out so great. We made our way to the beach, which isn't like any other Jersey shore. There's no boardwalks, or tourist traps with carnival rides and screaming children. It's a really chill place.

At the time, I didn't realize it, but both my grandparents owned nice houses on the island. I had been to my grandfather's house a few times when I was really little, and I went and stayed at my Grandmother's house 2 times when I was older and loved it. By the time I had graduated high school, my gramma said anyone in the family was allowed to use it at any time. Before I even got a chance to take her up on the offer, my younger cousin went, had a party and trashed the place. My Gramma was so pissed she was disrespected that she sold the place without even a second thought. She must have owned that house for decades and in one failed swoop, it was gone just like that. I never forgave her for ruining it for the rest of us.

Jane and I walked around the town, until eventually we met up with her friends who were renting an apartment there. Later that night we ended up at another kids house on LBI and this was huge. I mean it must have been big money to own this place. It was a regular mansion, and it was just blocks away from the beach. Not like a regular beachy vacation house. It felt like a real home. We walked in, and there were a few people there already drinking. Booze all over the kitchen island, I went and sat on the couch as I was already really uncomfortable since I was years away from being as mature as this group of kids.. Er ah young adults.

I was plopped on the couch, just trying to be invisible as more and more people started showing up. The Simpsons were on the television and I could have sat there all night. Jane came to check up on me, and eventually offered me some alcohol. Of course I said yes, even though I was way out of my league and super uncomfortable, I thought that maybe it would cheer me up, or at least numb all my insecurities. I drank, and drank, and drank. I started slurring my words, and I must have embarrassed Jane because she took me outside and tried to talk to me. We sat on the steps as she put her arm around me, and I tried to go in for a kiss. I was wasted, and all I wanted to do was to make out with her. She wanted nothing of the sort, and after I started to cry and become emotional, she convinced me that I just needed some rest. I agreed, and she escorted me upstairs into one of the bedrooms, where I laid down on top of the bedding of a single bed. I lay there rolled over staring at the wall, unable to sleep because of my drunkenness. That was always something that bothered me about being intoxicated, whether it be beer, or harder drugs. The fact that I couldn't voluntarily fall asleep when I wanted to literally drove me crazy. All you can do is think and think, thoughts racing, constantly unable to close your eyes. Acid was the worst for me as you take a trip and it would last up to 12 hours or more. When your body is tired, and your brain won't shut off, it makes for a very intense war between two worlds that are the same. This time was no different. I wasn't at blackout height yet, and I wasn't at pass out time yet. I lay there in trance unable to do anything about it. Time was my only friend.

I could have been laying there for hours, or I could have been laying there for minutes. Either way I started hearing a group of people make their way up the stairs, down the hall, and eventually they saw me and headed into the bedroom. There were 4 men, or young men rather, and they stood over top of me trying to figure out what kind of state I was in. Maybe they were off exploring the house, as people often do at parties, maybe they were looking for another bathroom since I am sure the other one downstairs would have been occupied and causing a line to form. Either way, they ended up there, with me laying on a bed incapable of moving.

One guy seemed particularly interested in me. It was hard to tell how tall he was, as I was laying down and could barely see straight a few feet away by that point, but he had curly dark hair and he didn't seem to be particularly tall. He started asking me questions to which each answer was a slur of words of some sort. Within a few minutes, they all knew I was in no shape to hold a conversation and they all thought it was hilarious. The one who found me interesting decided to grab me, and roll me over towards the side of the bed that wasn't near the wall, and drape my legs over towards him. Had I been sober, I would have been able to just sit up and put my feet on the ground. But instead, I lay there like a stiff. Incapable of moving my own body. Incapable of holding a conversation, incapable of doing anything that could ward off what this strapping young man was about to do to me. His friends still standing around him as if to cheer him on, he proceeded to undo my belt, and pull down my pants a little. In my mind I was screaming NO but nothing was happening and nothing seemed to come out of my mouth but silence. It felt like my lips were trying to move, but I felt like my soul was trapped inside my body, and my body was a foreign object.

With no objection from his buddies, he pulled my pants down even more and started to stroke my long pubic hair as he took his other hand to slide down his pants to which fell down to his shoes. He pulled me toward him more, and he raped me. I tried with all of my might to grab my pants and pull them up, but it was just impossible. I was so intoxicated that every move I made seemed impossible. Any time I would move my arm, he would grab it, pinning me down, and keep going. At first his friends all thought it was funny, one of them seemed to want to get in on the action as well, gently standing there waiting for his turn, while the other two disappeared. It seemed like it was going on forever but maybe that was just my drinking interpretation of it. Maybe it just felt like it was slow motion, because everything was going so slow. I am assuming the disappearance of the two other boys were the cause of Jane running into the room and pulling the guy off me. Thank you. Jane sat with me for a minute, realizing I was incapable of doing anything, she grabbed a few people to drag me down the stairs to her jeep, where she drove me back to the girls apartment, left me lying on a makeshift bed on the floor, and then went back to the party where she and her friends stay for the rest of the night until the early morning hours. I started to sober up at that time, as I lay there, in between 3 other girls on a floor where I could do nothing but think about what had occurred to me hours earlier. I didn't know it was possible to hate myself even more then at that moment. There is nothing worse than feeling violated sexually as a woman, and I was no stranger to it.

Jane never brought it up, we never talked about it. Now that I look back at it, I don't understand why no one called the police. Why didn't she at least talk to me about it, or help me to get help. Thank god I didn't end up pregnant, I wouldn't have any idea what to do with that. I didn't know that I probably should have gone to the hospital, or to the clinic. I had no knowledge of rape, or what should have been done in that situation. It's not something talked about. If you don't talk about it, then it doesn't exist. But that's bull, because it does exist, and it wasn't the only time it happened to me, sadly. I did blame myself for it. I did for a long time. But I know now that it wasn't my fault. It's hard to see that while you're going through it. It's just not something people can understand unless you live it.

The other time I was raped, yup, there was another, was actually by a friend. As if it wasn't bad enough that a stranger raped me, a neighbor molested me, and my mother abused me. This time was a few years later, when I was hanging out with this guy, again a few years older than me. I wouldn't have called him my boyfriend, because we weren't exclusive. He had many girls drooling over him, many of them mutual friends. But when we spent time together, I felt like I was the only one. He was a gentle giant of sorts. He was taller, and had some muscle build. Handsome in every definition of the word, and beautiful baby blue eyes.

We often spent time in his bedroom, listening to various punk and hardcore records. Blasting music loud so his mom couldn't hear us make out or roll around on the floor.

His room was quite large, as some sort of finished attic space that had angled walls and large windows in the front and back of the house. We lay on the floor talking and changing records as he started to make a move on me. I had no problem previously with making out with him though we had never had sex. But that day was a particular day that I was in no shape or form to be having sex. Being compromised with having my time of the month visiting, I politely declined to be making out. His attitude vastly changed in a blink of an eye, and he was very easily able to overtake me. He was probably a foot taller than me. And of course he had the muscle build to take 2 or 3 of me all at once. I said no, I pushed and shoved, and begged and pleaded. It was no use, and the blood was of no concern to him. He took what he wanted, and there was nothing I could do. At this point, I didn't even feel like I owned my own body anymore. It was just here to be used and tossed away and I hated it.

I hated everything. I hated everyone. I was filled with anger and hatred.

Eventually the beer, the 40's and wine coolers were just child's play and not even close enough to numb my pain. So I then started to move on to other things. Weed, shrooms, ecstasy, acid/LSD and angel dust were all added to my list of "drugs of choice". That's a phrase used frequently in rehab or NA meetings.

The first time I was asked " What's your drug of choice?" When I was in rehab and we went to a local group NA meeting (Narcotics anonymous) Everyone knew the protocol, except me. This was new to me at that time, especially since I wasn't a drug addict when I had even entered that facility. The person opening up the discussion would say his name "Hi I'm Tom" everyone would repeat back "Hi Tom"

"I am an addict"

And then the conversation or discussion would commence. It's customary for people to either tell their stories to the new people or have the new people introduce themselves. I have seen both happen. Me being a newcomer, I was asked to introduce myself.

I sat on a far end of a table, head buried into my arms, lying on the table trying to be invisible, as if I didn't belong there, but it didn't work. I said "My name is Jen, " to which everyone replied, "Hi Jen."

Someone had said that I needed to acknowledge that I was an addict, and I refused. Boy did that make things intense. I was in a room filled with sobering drug addicts who have done the hard time of self help and been through crap I could only imagine while some stupid kid sat in front of them claiming not to be an addict.

I refused to say I was an addict several times, until I started hearing crap from all sides. I finally gave in just to get people to leave me alone. "I'm an addict."

If they had only known the truth, I wonder what they would have had to say for advice. The first step in recovery is admitting you have a problem. At that stage in my life, I had yet to have a problem. Well at least I knew what was in store for me once I had formed a habit. Which I certainly started doing after being sexually taken advantage of..again.

Whatever was around, whatever was available, was what I would do. And the more drugs I did, the less I cared about what I was doing, how much I was doing, or who I was doing it with. When you're a drug addict, you think you have friends, but they aren't really your friends the same way you have friends when you are sober. Sober friends know your name, where you live. They know how old you are, what your favorite movies are, or maybe they know your favorite things to eat. You go to the movies together, you go to the park, you go to each other's houses and maybe spend time talking about daily bullcrap life things like school, work or siblings or parents.

Druggie friends know none of those things. I didn't even know the names of half the people I routinely did drugs with. Maybe I was introduced by name at one point in time, but no one ever pays attention to that. We pay attention to what you have, related to 2 things: drugs or money..or maybe a vehicle in which we then have a way to get the 2 previous items. We don't care what your name is, let alone what your favorite pizza toppings are.

Druggie friends all go to the same few spots. We know these spots, or also known as "places" are safe, away from cops or someone that may catch us doing said drugs. A major spot of mine was, believe it or not, the mall. Oxford Valley Mall. We were mallrats, in every sense of the word, I even quit my first job to work at the mall, a CVS so I could sell cigarettes to all my friends. One of the best spots at the mall was outside behind JCPenney. It was an area that was shown to me by some other druggie with no name, and I quickly found it to be my favorite. There was a loading dock, where all the tractor trailers would unload merchandise, but off to the side of the docks there was an empty storage container with a hole in the side of it. It sat there emptied and unscraped and the perfect hideaway for drug doing.

Usually the only thing we could do was smoke weed because it was always readily available. I would make bowls to smoke it out of the foil from the cigarette boxes. I am sure that was not a healthy way to smoke it, as people often came up with obscure things that would happen to you if you did drugs a certain way, but hell, I didn't give a crap. Before drugs, my friends and I even tried huffing gas, and doing "whip its" those came with heavy warnings too, that I completely ignored as well.

It's funny when I think about it now because it never seemed very hard to get drugs or buy drugs. All us "friends" always shared what we had, as druggies never liked to be alone while doing them. Especially more interesting stuff like acid and dust. No one ever wanted to be alone doing those things. It was just too fun, and the fun couldn't be contained by ourselves.

The first time you do a new drug you never know what to expect. Everyone has stories that sound great, hence the reason for the interest in them in the first place. But you really don't know for sure. Acid is no exception. It was the first new drug after weed and boy was it a nice change.

A friend from the street behind ours agreed we would try it for the first time together. We made plans to buy it off another kid in a park after school. We sat around waiting for her hook up, and after a few hours, started thinking that he was gonna flake out until through the woods we saw a figure coming in our direction. He waves us over to the tree lined area and then discusses buying 2 hits off him for 10$ each. A tiny square of perforated paper with a little stamped icon on it was our gateway to being high as a kite. He told us we had to put them on our tongues and let them dissolve, wait about an hour and you'll be tripping. Well we each wanted to wait for the other one to do it until we just did it at the same time. There it goes, dissolved away. Now all we had to do was wait for our ride to pick us up. Her parents were picking us up from the park and were supposed to take us home. We were bored of waiting for this tripping to start and thought that maybe it was just a hoax. Across the park we had spotted her parents van and we both looked at each other in terror as at that very moment we both started feeling the effects of the elucid drug known as LSD. We started freaking out, walking nice and slow to the van, trying to tell each other to walk normal, act normal. Just be normal or they will know!

All of a sudden we hear honking over and over again coming to the van and we start panicking. Are we walking in the right direction? What's going on? Why are they honking? She started yelling at me to run, and at that moment I tripped on my big pants and couldn't stop laughing. She looked at me with embarrassment and then started dying laughing herself. The honking was still going on so she started literally pulling me to the van by my pants, with my head dragging behind.

We get into the van and her parents say that we are going to Arby's for dinner.We sit in the back seats as her parents start driving out of the park and towards Arby's. No one ever wore seat belts back then, and we drug induced teenagers were no exception. As the van started turning and driving, we each fell out of the seats and ended up rolling around the floor dying of laughter. Her parents clearly looked annoyed, but didn't say anything to us. We get to Arby's and I just stare at the list of items that can be ordered. I had never been to an Arby's, and this being my first time, was a bad way to experience it. I stood there for at least 15 minutes while everyone already got and paid for food. Finally her mom just ordered for me as I quickly went to find a seat with everyone else. I couldn't eat it though. I tried. I picked up a fry and examined it for the entire duration of the stay there. What the hell did her parents think? I wish I knew. I don't really remember the rest of the night, but it must have been good because I wanted more of it.

I'll spare you from the details of every acid trip I took, but there were many. Too many to count. I started building up a tolerance to the stuff, and there was a rash of low potent stuff going around also because at one point I ended up doing 11 ½ hits at one time. The ½ obviously because I wasn't alone. Once I tried buying acid sugar cubes off a mall cop who was a frequent source of drugs, which turned out to be fake. I was so pissed because we had bought a whole bunch, and all it was was sugar cubes and nothing else. Serves me right.

Shrooms were fun, a nice cross high between weed and acid. But I'm not here to glorify drugs. Don't do them. I did them to numb my pain. Numb my life which I hated so much. I often thought of ways I could commit suicide. I always thought of hanging because it seemed easy and clean. I tried cutting my wrists but it was too scary, and hurt enough to make me stop from going any further. I was too chicken to do it. Years earlier in Elementary school a kid had killed himself with his dad's shotgun. I remember actually being jealous of him. He had suffered abuse at home, and had no other choice, or so he had thought at that young age.

Drugs were my life and the only thing I could rely on for a few years. I still maintained good grades at school, I still worked my job and was really good at it. I would never cross the worlds between each other, or so I thought I was better than that..until I wasn't. I started tripping at school, drinking before school, and then it started at my work.

I usually worked on the weekends constantly, and at one point I would work all night, take the bus from the mall into the city, party at raves all night, and take the bus or train back to work the next day still being high, and not have slept a wink.

I grew to love Philly during those days. I knew my way around the city without a map, I knew every bus and train route. Everything was easily accessible by either those or a taxi cab. I spent the entire weekends of my 11th and 12th grade high school year in Philly. Either sleeping at the train station waiting for the earliest R3 back home, wandering south street, raves or hardcore shows. I loved everything the city had to offer. It felt like an escape, it felt like it had no walls, yet so many places to hide.

9

Unplugged

My drug use became a part of my daily rituals. A friend that lived down the street ended up being a real partner in crime. We took turns buying drugs, and usually spent time at her place because it was nicer and her dad was always at work. One weekend we had dropped acid and with blacklights in hand, drew all over the entire house with highlighters. The colors of the walls were painted just the right tones of beige or browns that hid the highlighter colors just right in the daylight. But under the blacklights, the entire house lit up with graffiti, curse words and other obscure things that seemed to make sense to us at the time. Sarah was a very smart girl, and was at the very top of the class before becoming a druggie. I really think it was her need for attention from boys that got her started in doing them. Most of the druggies I hung out with were all boys, go figure. I never seemed to get along with females. Never have, and it's still the same to this day, though I am a totally different person now. Sarah and I had our own click of drugs, and one of them we used to call "Fat Tina" I mean, she called herself Fat Tina. She was a lot younger than us, and I don't even know how we became friends with her, she quickly became one of our favorite people to hang out with. Her mom drove us around everywhere, and actually bought drugs for us to do. She even insisted on feeding us and keeping us safe by doing drugs at her house. Her mom never did drugs, but I assume that something really bad happened to tara, that her mom felt responsible for. Either way, it worked in our favor. It was fun for a while, but I never felt comfortable at her house. Something to do with her mom always being there and catering to our every need that really made me uncomfortable. One night her mom was driving us around in the car, as I stared out the window on the rainy evening watching the raindrops fall down the side window, an announcement came over the radio.

Kurt Cobain was dead due to an apparent suicide. We all looked at each other in horror and I immediately started bawling my eyes out. April 8th 1994 Of course they then decided to play music from the entire Nirvana catalog. You couldn't get away from it, and I felt like my life was ruined. Music has played such a huge role in my life. Without it, I never would have gotten through life. Nirvana was no exception. Nirvana and the Cure were talking about things I felt that I lived with. It made my life seem important since other people were experiencing these things as well, and they were famous, so it couldn't be that bad right? I would cry listening to music, all the time. I had The Cures "Disintegration", It was my release when I needed to cry, I had hardcore music, Sick of it all, Quicksand, Lifetime or to be my release when I needed to get my anger out. I had Pink Floyd's "Wish you were here" When I often thought about my one true love that maybe one day I would meet. I had Morrissey's "girlfriend in a comma" which I actually would listen to while my mom was in her coma. There's different music for different emotions. Different songs remind you of different places, different people. Jim, my first real boyfriend, insisted our song was lady in red and insisted I wear a red dress when he took me to his senior prom. Music is a very powerful thing, so the death of someone you looked up to, or listened to on a regular basis was a tragedy. It also just so happened that we were all tripping on acid at the time they announced the finding of his body. It was no wonder that his death was so powerful that as the news started spreading, there were also increased reports of teen suicides that happened as a result. We all know he didn't kill himself.

Eventually, I started witnessing first hand Stacy's downfall, as her grades dropped and teachers started questioning her ability to even pass, I started to freak out a bit. We had fun for a long time but by the time I was about to start my last year in high school, I needed to find a change in scenery.

Watching Stacy's descent into drugs, and witnessing my own drop in grades, and then quitting my jobs, I suddenly realized that I needed to change or this would be my life. All my friends were always older than me and as they started to venture off into the real world, I would confide in the younger crowd at school around this time. I started dating 10th graders and hanging out with 10th graders. I loved it because I felt like I had control over them. They looked up to me and became "cool" as a result of being associated with me. Being cool was so stupid. Once I got to high school I stopped caring about it. I became friends with everyone. I never wanted anyone to feel the way I did growing up, I hated being made fun of or being called names. If I had ever seen anyone being made fun of, I took it upon myself to make sure it stopped. I did come a long way since torturing a school teacher.

I remembered people, places, and so I took action. I stopped everything cold turkey. I had to. At school when I was sober, I started getting increasingly paranoid. I also started having weird sensations in my body that were unexplainable and didn't have drugs to pin it on. I had lost control. I couldn't control what my body was feeling, or doing without enhancements, and I didn't like it at all. It made me feel like an alien inside myself and I wanted it to end. It took a long time for the side effects or whatever was happening to me to subside. After a few weeks of ignoring Stacy, I finally tried to confront her to see if I could get her to quit too. It was quickly apparent that I was more concerned about her life and future then she was. It had made me so upset that I couldn't help her. I lost a friend, and she couldn't care less to see me go...see that's a druggie friend for ya.

I decided to try to focus on myself, and get out of my mom's house. Everything became a countdown to graduation. I had no idea what I was going to do or where I was going to go, but I knew once I graduated, I was gone and would never come back.

My senior year I had short hair, that I had bleached and was growing out fast, I always had really dark roots. I always had hair clips pulling my short hair to the sides of my face. Piercings everywhere, 3 tattoos and I thought I was so unique. Well back then, I was. I was actually voted "Most Unique" in High school. Weird. I wasn't trying to be unique, but I certainly was a freak. I always felt like an outcast and this year was no different. Luckily I finally had a great friend that seemed to always like what I liked. Dressed how I wanted to dress. Pierced what I wanted. And eventually tattooed the same thing I had. We were best friends, and she was my first "real" BFF. Danielle and I were inseparable. But this chapter is not about our friendship.

One hot summer day in Langhorne Pennsylvania started out as a day trip with Danielle and I tagging along to her boyfriend and his family's day trip to Hershey Park. We all piled into a conversion van, Danielle, Jack, Kevin and I along with their mother and father. They had another brother, which I am assuming joined along but I have no recollection of it. Immediately after arriving at the park, we all went separate ways. Danielle and her boyfriend Jack, and then Kevin and I (who I had never met before) all ran around like the crazy lunatic teenagers we were. Kevin was a bit older than Danielle and I, Jack being a year younger than us, he was in the same grade and classes as my sister. That was all I had known of that family. Along with the fact that their mother was a school teacher and my sister had her at one point in her scholastic career. I knew they seemed like an all american family. They lived in a nice house, parents still married, one a school teacher and 3 boys with various years in between them.

I was really jealous when Danielle and Jack started dating. I mean, we were BFF..Best friends forever?! She was the only person I had in my corner. The only person wanting to spend time with me, and who I had fun with. But when she would make the hour-long trek to my house, she would let me take her car, and drop her off at his house. She would say, meet me back here (the corner near Jack's house) at "8 o'clock" and I would be there. Ummm with no license to drive of course. I wouldn't really do anything but wait around for her anyway- but at least I had the freedom to do so. Sometimes I would go to the 711 by my house and buy some cigarettes but that was about it. Of course I was 17 years old.

For some reason he didn't hang out much with just us two. We used to hang out the year before- when I was sort of dating Jake if you can call it that. It was a constant tug of war with him. We all (I mean the boys) all spend hours and hours after school skateboarding. I was always a tag along, and eventually Danielle was too. We bought skateboards, mine bore the photo of Drew Barrymore from a photo shoot from the Playboy issue. She was my idol. I loved her. For years I tried to look like her. Bleaching my hair, and curling it to make little ringlets like Shirley Temple. Drew Barrymore was so cute, and super freaking hot. All the guys loved and obsessed over her, and all the girls did too.

Danielle and I really tried hard to be good at skateboarding. We would go to the church parking lot in front of her house and just go back and forth. I could do 2 tricks that I learned by watching Jim, which I tried to teach Danielle, but with no guys ever taking us seriously enough to show us anything, we were bound to drop the boards real quick. I only ever used mine for transportation once I moved to Philly, but after wiping out a few times because the sidewalks and roads were so screwed, I gave it up and switched to a bike instead.

Back to said amusement park. We had fun running around the park, getting kicked out of the karaoke booth for probably being annoying. We played games, won stupid stuffed animals and whatever. On the way home, Kevin and I fell asleep in the back of the van on the floor together. Wiped out from the hot sweaty day running around, eating junk food and pretending life was great. We were inseparable for days after that. Then days turned into weeks. I really liked his kind heart. He was such a loving, kind, gentle soul. His face was soft, and his eyes just glowed and I got lost in them like he was the cutest baby beagle puppy I had always longed for. Eventually he fell in love with me. We had sex..of course, and then he became obsessed with me. In my young, naive age, I got really tired and annoyed with him real quick. I broke up with him after that while he was at my house. After I had sex with someone, I felt nothing for them. I just wanted to run away and pretend nothing happened, or pretend they didn't exist. A result of my traumas.

My way of communication was always writing. I had written it down in my notebook and gave it to him. We often wrote poems together, and expressed our hatred for life together. He wrote something in my notebook, cut his wrist and proceeded to wipe his dripping blood all over the pages. Over our month or 2 of being with each other everything, I had started to realize just how unstable Kevin was. The more I withdrew from him, the worse he started acting. And this was just the beginning of me knowing him. Eventually Danielle and I started seeing less and less of each other.

One day his brother Jack called me and said I had to come over right away. Kevin had a knife and wanted to kill himself. I had to go over and calm him down. I remember going over to their nice house, walking through the huge addition they had added to the house, and seeing Kevin all huddled up in the backyard near a shed, hiding. He just stood there with a knife to his wrist. He just wanted to end his life. I felt like it was all my fault.

Once school started I saw him in the 1st period. We both took screenprinting and though we had different teachers, the workshops were connected and the large doors were always opened towards the adjoining room. We sat there- desks facing each other and never saying a word. Every week I would look up across the room and see his face. Always looking depressed and tired. When I couldn't look up and see his face, it would be pressed to the side lying there on the cold hard desk. He would be sleeping in class more than he would participate. It was a shame, because it really was one of the highlights of High school for me. We made business cards, thank you cards embossed with gold and silver ink. We created logos and designed notepads which we printed and cut ourselves. We created t-shirt designs, mine being lyrics to a Bikini Kill song on the back and the logo on the front. In true "Riot Grrrl" fashion, that couldn't be bought at the local Gap.

Whenever we had a free moment, I always went over to talk to him. He would usually ignore me, and stay asleep, but other times we would talk with light conversations. He had a few girlfriends after me, but he never acted like a close friend to me again. He would say hi to me, I would get excited for him about a girlfriend because then it meant he wouldn't think about hating me so much. But it never really seemed to work. I really tried so hard to be friendly to him. I could tell I broke his heart. If only he had acted like he didn't care about me, we would be in a different situation. I saw a play he did in theatre, and that was really the only time I had seen him actually look like himself. I was so proud of him, and it looked like he really enjoyed it. I'm glad he seemed to find something to do that wasn't related to love..or me.

A few months later, in April 1996 Danielle called me and told me Kevin had died of a heroin overdose. Truthfully, I didn't even know he had done drugs, or was that far deep in it. From what I understand he had 30 days sober. He and some friends went to South street to celebrate his sobriety. His friends went to see a show at JC Dobbs and he either couldn't get in or decided not to go in because he didn't like the band playing. Whatever the situation, he ended up walking up and down the street alone. Which is dangerous for anyone at night, but more so a young man with only 30 days clean. Back then, we spent a lot of time down in Philly. It was a short ride on the R3 train and then a hike straight down to the coolest street in the city. Back then it was all punk kids, people either looking for or selling drugs, and tourists. Oh, and don't forget the Hare Krishnas. More on them later. It wasn't uncommon for someone to walk by you and say "weed" or "acid/trip". This is how they looked for buyers. If you repeated what they said "Weed?" then they would quickly turn around and engage in a conversation with you about how much you were looking for. Yes, I have bought many things from south street vendors. Not by myself of course.

There he is, Kevin, walking up and down South Street. What was he thinking? Apparently he went down the wrong alley way, scored some heroin which was his drug of choice. Went home, got in some sort of a fight with his mom probably to keep her away from his room and proceeded to do heroin for the rest of the night. His brother found him the next morning dead while choking on his own vomit. A tragic terrible fate for this wonderful human being that had so much to offer this world, yet felt like he was nothing. I sadly didn't know anything that weighed so heavy on his mind that he felt like drugs were the only answer. I missed a day of school. I just couldn't understand his death at all. I would have stayed home longer but my mom just got pissed, so uncaring about my ex boyfriend and friend losing his life. I felt like it was partially my fault, like if I had just stayed with him maybe he would still be alive. It had been only 10 months since the first time I had ever met him, which in teenage years was like a decade. I don't have that kind of power.

The funeral was awkward to say the least. I remember wearing my vintage clothes and my freakish look- and feeling so out of place. I had on my favorite maroon coat that had a huge black fur collar. Maybe I only remember because I got so many compliments on it that night. It's a funeral, shouldn't I look "normal" I thought. I had never been to one before so I didn't really know the right way to be. There were lots and lots of people there. I really didn't understand it. Hundreds of people at a funeral for a teenage kid who only felt like he was all alone. Was it just because his mom was a school teacher? I don't know any of these people. It was a really long line. I felt like I was in line for hours waiting for my turn. The line literally went out of the room, down the hall, down the front steps and into the street. When I say hundreds of people, I was not exaggerating. I ended up talking to the girl in front of me. Turned out to be one of his ex girlfriends, after me. Though she said they still were friendly with each other. She annoyed me and I was stuck talking to her. She was tall and thin which was the most annoying. We ended up hanging out a few times after that and I ended up making a new batch of messed up friends.

I remember walking up to the casket and not realizing it until I went into shock that it was an open casket. My first funeral, my first dead body. So pale and empty inside. I looked at his face, touched his hand, and placed my letter next to his body along with all the other trinkets people had placed there. I had written pages upon pages of words expressing how sorry I was that this happened, along with a picture of us together. He had been only 2 months shy of graduating high school.

In response to his huge love for the theatre group and acting, the high school ended up naming the auditorium after him. I always said that once I started to make good money I would donate money to the school drama club in memory of him. But here I am 20 years later and still trying to live week to week. Kevin's death really made me realize how fragile life was. You never know what someone is going through, at any given point in their life. It made me think about how I had impacted his life. I would never know if I had done something different, if he would have still been here. I had always been able to talk to him, to calm him down, to see a better side to depression. Because I was in it too. But at 17, I had never really talked about those types of things. The things that make me depressed. To give credit, I don't really think I thought about them either. Or really even understood the impact that the male personalities in my childhood had affected me for the rest of my life. I am sure it was partly true for Kevin too. Though I don't know what his demons were. And we all do have our own demons to deal with.

Kevin wasn't the only one I felt like I had ruined. I had an admirer who followed me around everywhere in college. He tried hard to be my boyfriend, but when I declined he just wouldn't leave me alone. I tried everything, I made up excuses but nothing would give him the idea to leave me alone. He started leaving weird letters in my mailbox and then when he showed up at my house, I just said the first thing that came to my mind. I said I wouldn't date him because he had no tattoos. It was the only thing I could think of, which was a total lie but he finally couldn't contest it. He didn't have any tattoos. Years later when I was at a tattoo convention, I ran into him. I didn't remember him, but he sure remembered me. "You're the reason I became a tattoo artist." He said to me, I really had no idea how to react to him when I had realized who he was. It was very awkward, and I stayed on the other side of the convention in hopes of not running into him again.

I think I ruined every relationship I had ever had. The second a boy would treat me well, I quit. I got bored. I liked being treated like crap. I liked when they didn't act like I existed. I liked being ignored. Even worse was that I loved sex. And not to feel connected with someone, but just for the actual physical pleasure. I liked to be hurt, it was the only thing I ever knew. It was comfortable. Anything else was foreign to me and so anything remotely "normal" and I immediately tried to sabotage it. I was very successful at sabotaging. I hope you are starting to see the patterns. Seeing the patterns is the first step in recovery. Just like in NA or AA. Recognition or admission are the first steps. It still took me years to notice the patterns of destruction.

10

At The Drive In

The rest of my senior year was a total blur. I did what I had to do, I had a work permit to leave school early, and I was doing so well and ahead of the game that I was taking a college level course, whatever the hell that means. My focus by then wasn't academic though, it was for art and photography. I had taken photographs for the duration of my time in high school as an elective and art as well, but photography just came totally natural to me. It didn't hurt either that I could hide in the darkroom all class and smoke cigarettes, or take an assignment, wander around the school with a free pass for exploration. Poor Mrs. Ziggy. I got tons of crap over on her. I actually had a real love for her. She showed me kindness despite the rare occasion of me acting out. I always seemed to hurt the ones I loved. Something I learned. I think a small part of her knew I had problems at home. She had told us about a contest for a full paid scholarship at the Art Institute of Philadelphia. They had the contest once a year and the requirements were for 12th graders to submit a portfolio consisting of matted/ framed prints, one from each category given, and then an essay. I had spent the better half of my time photographing and developing prints and negatives for this portfolio contest. It was my only way out of town. My mom constantly argued with me about what I was going to do after graduation, how I couldn't stay there, and how I wasn't wanted. She reminded me how she had no money to pay for my college, and she wasn't going to help me in any way, whatsoever. As soon as you graduate, there's no more child support and you are done living here. Constantly being reminded how I was only there because she was getting paid. I had already been paying for all my own clothes and food for years by then so I didn't see why she would think I would even think to ask her for help in the first place. Most of my friends opted for community college but it wasn't very close. Of course not as far as Philly was, but you needed a car to get to community college, and that just looked like a huge other block on my way out of town. I still didn't have a license to drive.

I always had a really great work ethic. I think it was from having to grow up at such a young age. Every job I had I took seriously and I knew that my only way out was with my own 2 feet, and I had to find my feet for myself.

I took every dollar I had, I found a new job at Neshaminy mall, I spent every minute taking pictures, or getting ready for that contest. The one thing I had a really hard time with was the essay. I didn't know what to write. The question had something to do with me, with I. That was something I totally didn't connect with. I blew it off until it ended up being the last day for entries. The very last day. I asked my mom to drive me to philly, to the school to drop it off and she wouldn't do it. She refused to help me. Are you surprised? I mean, really. I called around until I finally found someone that would help me and to this day, I still thank him for helping me. For driving me a half hour through the pouring rain just for me to drop off the essay and the portfolio. I wrote the essay while I was waiting for him to pick me up. I jotted down what I thought was the best thing. I really didn't like it, but what I wrote was the truth, and that's all I could do to feel complete about it.

I had gone to an open house and to a week-long session at the Art Institute of Philadelphia right before that, so I was already familiar with the school. I also had made friends there, and had frequently partied at the dorms years earlier. I made lots of "boyfriends" and had made my way sleeping through many of the various majors offered there. But by the time I had found out that I had won the full paid scholarship, I became really nervous about attending the school. I didn't want to live in the dorms, and it was a requirement before being able to live at any of the other housing they offered. You were free to live in a rented apartment, but I was 18, no one would rent me a place and government loans wouldn't have covered it unless I had roommates to split the bills with anyway. For months I worried about how my sobriety would be affected from living in that place, and I had a reason to be afraid.

I never got recognition for anything I did. Whether it was all the bad crap I did, or something worthy of praise like getting a free ride to college. So when the high school asked the students if they had any announcements for scholarships, or money awards for us for college, I didn't even hesitate to write down my achievement. I was so happy that I had done something right, and that I was actually trying to turn my life around. All I wanted was for someone to show they cared too, or even just a pat on the back. So the announcements came on, and they totally missed my name, and my announcement.

I went to the office to rectify it. At actual graduation the same announcement, and this time, I tried to make sure they added it in and got it right. Not only did they get my name wrong, they got the award of a full paid scholarship wrong as well. To top it off, the name they wrote on my diploma was spelled wrong. It never got spelled right, ever. Jenifer with one lonely N.

Not Jennifer, Jenniffer, Jessica. Throughout my life I would say my name and people called me Jessica. I never understood it. In fact it became so annoying that in the past few years I started ordering food as Jessica. Do I have some sort of lisp when I talk? It's Jenifer. I hated being called Jen or anything other then what my birth name actually was.. Why, why is it spelled that way? My mom's excuse was that my dad was drunk when he wrote it on the birth certificate at the hospital and that he was a terrible speller. My dad says he did it on purpose because he knew I was special. The thing that gives me a headache every time someone asks what my name is, regardless of whether I had to spell it or not. The universe was showing me just how big my identity crisis was internally.

I was so happy when I was at the end of my career in that school. I always felt more mature than all the other kids, even the older ones. Everyone was so serious about school work and their "permanent" record, but I saw past all that. I knew life was bigger than SAT scores, which I wasn't allowed to take because my mom wouldn't pay for it. Luckily, I didn't need test scores for Art school. Everything in school seemed so miniscule compared to the bigger picture of life. Perhaps that was because I had real life problems, when everyone else had stupid problems that in the end didn't mean anything. Either way, I was glad to be done with it.

I graduated in the beginning of June of 1996, and 2 weeks later I started classes at AIPH. I had no great summer vacation, I had to move on with real life and grow up even more. Everything I owned was packed up or thrown out except for a bunch of mementos or things not needed or things that wouldn't fit in my dorm room. Along with my 18th year old birthday gifts..tupperware and a cookbook. I got the hint mom. She couldn't wait for me to be out of the house.

It took one car trip and my mom dropped me off at the dorms. Her and Simpson helped me load things in, as I met a nice boy named Aaron. He was really cute, and offered to show me around or answer any questions I had. He was Vegan and straight, and I knew we would get along great. All my stuff was out of my moms car, and a quick goodbye, and a pack of food stamps in hand, and she left, and I couldn't have been more happy to see her go. My first quarter away at college and it was all me, myself and I.

I wish I could say this was the beginning of the healing. But it wasn't. My fears of getting into trouble when I moved into the dorms were quickly realized as my habits and problems with addiction quickly came back as if they had never left me. Just hibernating until that perfect weak moment where it pounced on me like a ton of bricks and I just had to submit because I wasn't as strong as I thought I was.

I was able to get my own room and didn't have to share because well, most people didn't like to start school in June. Of course I was an exception. I couldn't wait to get the hell out on my own. I had no one to hold my hand. I had no one to tell me what I should look for, or how to live in a big city, or even how to live by yourself when you're only 18 years old. But the truth was, I had been taking care of myself since I was at least 8, though I would argue that it was much earlier, so I had plenty of experience already. My schooling was paid for by the scholarship, and I had gotten a loan to help pay for school supplies, and a very small grant that also helped with paying for living expenses. But majoring in a subject like Photography- in the 90's was a very expensive bill. This is before digital photography, so we did everything with film and image developing. All these expenses added up, especially at the end of each quarter when you would have major projects due. But in the beginning I didn't really know what it was going to be like. I was handed a big fat check, which I had to somehow make last for like 6 months until I got the next check. I looked at it and thought, there is so much money here, this has got to be a mistake. I mean in reality it was probably like 800$. Even in the 90's that's not a lot of money to live on for 6 months. When I didn't get arrested at the bank for a fraudulent check, I was so relieved, and then I headed off to get supplies.

The first few months were brutal, I partied so much, I barely ever slept at all, and to top it off I almost flunked a class. It was the first class in the mornings, it was with a teacher who had this voice that literally made me fall asleep everyday, and it was for Photo Techniques which was so boring. I mean, I hated the actual science of photography. Which is why I don't have a high paying job in photography. I loved it for the art and expression of it, and nothing else. Portraiture was my favorite, and I seemed to be exceptionally gifted at environmental portraits. I always loved being behind a camera, and still do. I hate having my picture taken, I really don't know why. I think because I hated to be seen.

I quickly made friends of all sorts living in the dorms. A few girls, but a lot of boys...of course. We drank a lot, smoked weed once or twice until my paranoia came back, and I vowed to never do drugs again. I stuck to drinking as it seemed I was able to control it more. Or at least I thought I could. We learned the ways of getting beer, and sneaking it up to our rooms. There was a liquor store near south street that was dubbed the "Cop Shop" Apparently it was owned by cops. So either it was owned by cops and they thought no one in their right mind would ever attempt to buy underage there, or because they were cops, they had a blind eye to underage drinking. Either way, it was a hit every time, never asking for ID. Not once. We would cover it with a jacket, or some laundry and sneak it up in the elevator and down the hall to our rooms. We would mask it by putting it in soda cans, or coffee cups.

The building that housed the dorms was very unique. I have been to other college dorms like Kutztown which had one bathroom on the whole floor, which were all girls but it was nothing like where I lived. First off, it was coed. Which is bad enough. But the building used to be a Best Western Hotel. So we had our own bathrooms, the rooms were a real decent size, and there were full kitchens with lounge areas on each floor. And the floors were really small. Maybe like 15 rooms to a floor. The only thing that was the same was that if you were a girl, you had a girl roommate. But across the hall and next door might be rooms with boys. We pretty much all mingled except for one room with 2 super nerdy gamers. They played video games all night and never left their room. I tried making friends with them because I was always trying to meet new boys. They weren't interested. I made friends with the first gay guy i had ever met. He was so obviously gay, not to sound stereo-typical, but I had a gaydar and it was going off. I really became close with him, and we always spent time together. He told me how he had a crush on another person that lived on our floor and should have kept that secret to myself. Problem was that the person was trying to put the moves on me, and he wouldn't take no for an answer and so I ended up telling him about my close friend's crush on him. Of course he wasn't supposed to say anything, but as gossip goes, it came back around. My friend never talked to me again, and was totally crushed as he didn't even want a single person to know he was even gay. I wasn't trying to blow up his spot. I have always felt terrible about the whole situation, especially since he was probably a good 10 years older than everyone else. He wasn't ready to come out, and it ended up not being his choice that he did. In the 90's living as a homosexual was not easy. But it didn't seem like a big deal to me who did what. I never gave a care what people thought of me. I think for the most part it was because I had a big attitude problem, but there always seemed to be something inside of me that was more mature than the age that I was. I can't really explain it in words but I have always felt like I had lived more than once.

Philly had a neighborhood known as the self proclaimed "Gayborhood" It had rainbow flags on the street corners, it had a gay pride parade every year, and it was a testament as to how Philly seemed to be less affected by the discrimination that the rest of the country seemed to have. Perhaps because I myself had sexual relationships with women, that I didn't take into consideration my friend's feelings about his own sexuality. He didn't take the whole situation well, and decided to get revenge on me, which he did. He spread rumors and lies about me, which did seem to cause problems, but I did my best to remain neutral and not let it affect me. Of course it did affect me, and no matter how many times I apologized to him, he still never was as good a friend to me as he was before. We certainly learn a lot from how we act towards other people in relationships only I was just too dumb to realize it back then.

Anyway, as I started to become alienated from him and some other people, I started to realize that I needed to find other people to hang out with. Around Christmas time, most of the students started trickling back home for the 2 week break we had. I ended up being the only person living in the dorms, by myself, for a whole 2 weeks. It got really boring for a while until I started inviting friends from back home to come visit me. One night 2 boys ended up coming over and so I found another girl from the area to hang out with so it wasn't weird. We bought a bunch of 6 packs and drank all night being as loud as we wanted to. There was an eerie silence on the empty floors as we ran around the place acting like a bunch of kids. Eventually, I became so intoxicated that I dragged the one boy to my bed and he lay down next to me. The poor kid had no idea what he was in for. I do remember trying to make out with him, and he was a bit standoffish. In my drunken attempt to persuade him, I decided to totally strip down to my underwear and get in bed with him. That's all I remember because I blacked out the rest. When I woke up, I found myself naked, and with my clothes in a pile on the floor and the bed next to me cold and empty. I talked to him the next day and he told me that I begged him to have sex with me until eventually passed out and him and his friend left. I was so embarrassed by the whole situation that I never talked to him again. We didn't have cell phones back then, our only way of contacting people was one pay phone at the end of the hall. I did have a pager though, if you know what that is. Many of you probably will not. The rest of the vacation, I stay in the dorms, locked up by myself eating Ramen noodles and veggie burgers with no bread and juice boxes. Once school started back up again, I went on a tear. I slept with probably half of the boys on my floor. Some of them, I never actually had sex with, but would crawl in bed with them and just literally sleep next to them. There were 2 roommates, both named Dave that I did that with. We all felt lonely very often, and it was more of a loving, brother sister type of relationship. We took care of each other and whenever the other would be sad or lonely, we would go looking around to find each other. I even turned to the same sex. I had a full fledged girlfriend named Tara. She worked at the school which was where some of the majors needed to rent equipment. We used it to rent enlarger lenses for the darkroom, and you could get things to develop with and what not. She just so happened to show interest in me, and I obliged. I was only in it for the sex though, and she fell a lot harder than I did. I had only had sexual relationships with women, and not an actual girlfriend. She always called me her girlfriend, and showed up wherever I was, and totally smothered me. People would ask if we were dating and I denied it for a while. Eventually people knew what was really going on because we were always together. We did things sexually that I had never done with my fake drunk girlfriend, and I enjoyed receiving it, but didn't enjoy giving it. I think I had realized that maybe I wasn't a lesbian, though I was more attracted to the female body. I really just wanted a man's love and attention more. I had to eventually let her down nicely, and I really tried to remain friends with her, but it was always so awkward. It took another decade before I understood my own feelings and emotions pertaining to women, thankfully I have been able to resolve them.

There was one friend that started having a real problem being away at college. He was a hercin addict. There were 2 of them actually, but I never really hung out with the one kid. My friend was having a really hard time. He couldn t stay sober, and started flunking. He was in such a deep dark place that he couldn't find his way out alone. One night I saw him in the hallway pacing and looking very frantic. I tried talking to him, and he eventually just totally broke down. We sat in his room as he begged me for help. I had no idea what to do. He was going to fail and if he failed, he would have to go back home and his parents would know he has a problem. His parents were paying for school, and as long as he got good grades, he was allowed to get a free ride. He knew he needed help getting off heroin so he could get back to what was important to him, but he couldn't get off drugs by himself, and he knew that. He begged for my help, and so the only thing I could think of was to call a rehab to get him admitted.

Some numbers were just answering machines, some people wouldn't even talk to me, while finally I got a person on the phone that sounded like they were willing to talk. They informed me that he could be admitted but needed his parents to do it, as he was a minor. He couldn't let his parents know he was getting treatment. We had a real problem, with no solution. No one was willing to see him, or even try to help him without his parents. I was furious and felt like the system really let him down. Maybe it was the way it was supposed to happen though. I can't really say because I am not him, and after he did flunk out, I never saw him again. It was a shock to me and so after all this crap I did to myself and other people, it was about time I did some changing. I stopped drinking, no drugs, and stopped sleeping with every boy that showed an interest in me.

I started hanging out with my friend Danielle again from back home. She was sober, and the best person for me to be spending time with. But it didn't last long, as she ended up falling for the other kids down the hall addicted to heroin. As soon as I started seeing her at the dorms with him, and not even telling me she was there, I knew it would not end well. I begged and pleaded with her to stop seeing him. But anything I did only seemed to push her away further. I started noticing changes in her from afar, and I knew she had been converted to an addict...again.

Now Danielle and I had met in high school, and we hung out for a while, but her parents never liked me. When Danielle started mirroring my punk look of either green or fire engine red or hot pink hair, and then tattoos, and really odd clothing choices, they thought I was setting a very bad example for their daughter. I was always sober when Danielle and I were friends coincidentally, so if looking different is really a bad example, then I guess I was guilty of that. But looks never mattered to me, it was always the inside that counts, as cliche as it sounds. My heart, though often veered off track, was always trying to come from a true place of love. Danielle ended up moving into the dorms, and so I did everything I could to try to get her in trouble. I wanted them to be separated in order to save her but nothing worked. I called her parents and told them where she was and what she was doing but they were always so timid in disciplining her. When that went nowhere, I went down to the school office and told them there was a girl living in the dorms that wasn't a student and that they were doing hard drugs. They did nothing and within a few weeks, they both disappeared. Fast forward like 2 or 3 years and she calls me out of the blue. She called to tell me her boyfriend died of a heroin overdose and she was now in rehab in another state. Having a brother already died from a drug overdose, and now this, I'm surprised she hadn't learned anything from it. Not to mention our friend Kevin from high school. She knew where this led. Heroin does not lead to a great fantastic life. It leads to death. It was only a matter of time and I honestly didn't feel bad for her.

There are a lot of nice things I would say about her, but there's a lot that hasn't been pleasant. We ended up having a really great relationship as adults when we ended up having kids only a few months apart. Her parents were my parents. They were the only ones I ever felt cared about me. They grew to love my kids and knew that I really wasn't a bad in-fluence after all. I was one of the good ones...at least I was while I was friends with their daughter. I never had female friends last very long. Women have a habit of getting jealous and that was not something I was ever fond of. But eventually our friendship had ended by a strange twist of her personality.

Every now and then I would drop by to see Aaron, the Vegan straight edge kid I met on the first day of moving in. He had seen the tattoos that I had on my arms and wanted to introduce me to his friends that tattooed on south street. Tattoos were always a part of my childhood. Seeing bikers in the bar, or at my house, they all would be covered. I had a fascination for them and had always dreamed of being a tattoo artist. My true passion. If I had a choice, I wanted to go to Art School, The University of the Arts, a real art school. And then eventually learn how to tattoo. But I didn't have a choice as I had no support.

When I was 15 my mom asked me what I wanted for my birthday, and I said a tattoo. Her friends owned a tattoo shop, of course, and so he actually came to our house and we had a tattoo birthday party. It con-sisted of all my mom's friends getting tattoos at our dining room table until it was my turn. I had no friends at the party. I had my mind set on getting my favorite band's logo. "Black Train Jack" They had a song in particular that I always identified with and they were by far my favorite band. I had seen them play a million times at City Gardens since they were from NY/NJ and it was the only thing I wanted tattooed, and I had been thinking about it for years. My mom would not let me get it no matter how much I begged. She was the one paying for it after all, and her excuse was that I would like that band when I'm older. I still listen to them to this day. I opted instead for a tribal sun. I was obsessed with suns and moons. I don't really have a reason why, but they have always been a part of me. When I came into school at age 15 with a tattoo, a real tattoo on my arm, I thought I oozed coolness. Not like I cared though. I didn't give a crap about what people thought in reality. But once you have one tattoo, it was very easy for me to get more and more. I had 4 or 5 by the time I went away to college, even though I had just turned 18. Once I had met Aaron's friends, and he himself was covered in tattoos, I decided to use all my spare money to get more.

I was really self conscious about my arms growing up because they were covered in scars. All from the abuse caused by my mom. She had these huge, thick long nails which were always painted bright red. Whenever we acted up, especially out in public, her way of getting us to stop was by grabbing our arms and digging her knife-like nails into my skin until they bled. If I made a noise, she would dig deeper and deeper. I wouldn't be surprised if her sole purpose in having those nails was to keep me in line. It worked, but that didn't mean it was only a few times. If she didn't like how slow I was walking, it was the nails to drag me. If I was mean to my sister, it was the nails. Those 10 nails were so thick that you could see little crescent moon shaped scars going up and down the inside of my arms. My sole purpose for getting my arms totally covered with tattoos in the span of a year was only to cover the scars left behind by physical abuse. I had only ever said that outloud twice in my whole life and one was very recent as I started to shed layers of the shell that the abuse had made over top of me. After I covered my arms with tattoos, I started on a back piece. I ended up getting a Japanese dragon that took a really long time to finish. I wanted it because I had done a lot of reading on the culture, and getting a dragon on your back was a form of protection. I needed protection, and was willing to go through the pain in order to feel I had it.

The problem that ended up happening was that it actually caused me to get more attention which I wasn't planning on. I hated when people would walk up to me, grab my arm and stare at it and talk to me about them. This was before there were so many tattoo shows on TV. Not a lot of people, let alone women walked around with full sleeves tattooed. Today it's a pretty much normal way of life. But back then it was very rare. What made it even worse was that my dad was so ashamed of me that He refused to be seen in public with me without long sleeves to cover them. I once visited him in Florida and I had to wear long sleeves in 80 and 90 degree weather. The universe has a way of balancing things out, or you can call it Karma. Years later when he was visiting me, I wore my long sleeves as we went out to eat at Nifty Fifty's diner, and the waitress came over and spilled my dad's tall glass of soda all over me. After cleaning up in the bathroom, I had no choice but to take my sweater off. My dad knew then that God was showing him a sign to get over it with humor, and he did.

By this time, I had no contact with anyone in my family for a really long time. I had moved out of the dorms, tried living in North Philly until 3 months went by and almost died every time I left my place , so I finally ended up living a block from south street. It was a great trinity apartment, meaning it had 3 floors (and a finished basement) and one room on each floor. I had a dominatrix that lived next door for a while before she moved to a bigger city, a group of really cute skaters on the other side of me, and two old school punk drug addicts living next door to them. It was a really odd scene for sure. The landlords owned a pager store down the street, and I would often see the middle aged son around the building doing odd jobs. I do believe he was also "off" . I often noticed my toilet seat would be up, when I only lived with another girl. I often saw things move out of place, and also saw him leaving other neighbors' houses. My one neighbor said she caught him in her house, and he said he was facing the kitchen sink..which did not need to be fixed. I had lived there for a little while, and my roommate had ended up moving out. My sister often called me while I was away at school. I had left her with my mom. There was no one to stick up for her. My sister would call me and complain about her, and eventually my mom would call me and I was always in the middle trying to resolve everything. I was the mediator, and the parent, even though I was miles away and really tried to distance myself from them.

I went back to my mom's house about a year after I had moved out and went up to my room to get something, and as I walked in, I was overcome with a huge sense of sadness. The room that was my bedroom for many years had been converted into my mom's "office" and sewing room. There was no bed there anymore, nowhere for me to sleep if I wanted to come home and visit. It was as if I never existed. My mom later told me that she started working on it immediately after I had moved out. And she had thrown out everything that I had left behind. It was just a huge heartbreak to me, even if I didn't want to come back, the fact that she had shown no emotion about me being gone, just made it even worse.

The more time that went by, the more depressed I started getting. I had a job, and was busy with school, but I just started feeling like life was never going to get any better. I had lots of self pity, and it seemed to only fuel the fire. I tried having boyfriends and relationships, but I always either ruined it, or would get cheated on. At one point, every boyfriend I had for months cheated on me. I didn't want to be alone because I didn't know what to do with myself except be depressed. One particular break up really screwed me up for a long time. But it did teach me a huge lesson.

After all the crying, and talking crap about him around the city, I started to reflect back on my life. I realized that in order to move on with my life, I needed to have forgiveness. I ended up writing a letter to my mom which was like 10 pages long. It contained all my hatred and anger towards her, but by the end, it was a letter forgiving her for all that she had done to me. I never actually sent it to her, instead I shoved it in a random book and have since thrown it out I think. Either way, it was a huge weight that was lifted off my shoulders. I did the same for the boyfriend that I caught cheating on me, and it had the same effect. I soon realized after that, if I wanted someone to love me, truly love me, that I would have to love myself first.

Eventually, I ended up living alone, and found contentment with that. I didn't need anyone else to make me happy. I spent my time alone at home either listening to music, or just writing in journals or poems. I was healing myself the only way I thought of. And it did help me. It really helped me. I had never read any self help books, but this knowledge seemed to come from a higher power. I just felt it within myself, and as long as I was open to the path, I could see which way to go. I was close to ending my time at college, about to graduate and I had no idea where I was going or what I was going to do again. What I really wanted to do was transfer to another school in another state, still hoping to go to Art school. But I vowed that the universe and God would take care of me. During our portfolio review which serves as a way for people to look for new talent, I was an obvious overlooked candidate for many jobs. My images really set themselves apart from my peers. I focused on portraits, environmental portraits, and most of them were of drug addicts who may or may not have been high at the time. There was an obvious focus on the female body, and could have been a documentary for people who lived on the streets. There were a number of photographs that were even the opposite. I had women that were dressed very dignified, and then I had a few men in there as well, but even I could tell the difference between the intimacy of the subjects and myself. I had a way of making people feel comfortable. I had certain tricks I would do, as to distract them from what we were actually doing. It was and is the only way to get great pictures where the subjects are not being "posed" A posed subject lacks heart. It is just a moment in time that was captured where you pretend to be happy, or pretend that everything is fine, so someone else can look at and not think anything of it. What's the point in that? A picture is a story, as the cliche goes, a picture tells a thousand words. But what do the family album pictures say? The one where you're on a mountain top smiling at the camera? Does it say how much you sweat hiking up the mountain, does it tell the story of why, when and how you came up the mountain? It doesn't. There's a way to tell a story, and I happened to be very good at it. Unfortunately I lacked complete confidence in myself, and I was deathly afraid of ever walking into an interview. All my trauma had weighed so heavily on my shoulders that I wasn't even really aware of how it had all affected me so much. I really tried not to worry about anything and just let the universe take the wheel. By the actual graduation and the end of the month, I had to move out of my apartment. I didn't want to sign a new lease since I didn't know where life was going to lead me. I had just recently started dating someone, who loved to act like I did not exist, so naturally it was the perfect relationship for me. When they say you end up with people who remind you of your parents, they really are telling the truth. We get comfortable in patterns, whether it's bad or good patterns is another story. Not having any job offers, I decided to ask him if I could move in with him. I mean, I was already at his apartment all the time anyway because it was a lot closer to school. It was in the heart of the gayborhood which I explained earlier. 13th and Locust became my new home, as he allowed me to move in for the sole fact that he was leaving school to start his career and go out on the road touring with a band for 3 months. He needed someone to take care of his cat and be there to pay his bills. So naturally it became a perfect situation for both of us. We had only been dating for a few months, if you even want to call it dating, but living with each other seemed way too serious for either of us. This just seemed to be a way of helping each other out and less about moving to the "next level"

I move in, he goes out on tour to document life on the road, and I end up adding another job to my day as a photo lab technician. It was a really great job, and I made pretty good money. I processed all the negatives and printed all the photographs for a lab in center city that had 2 locations. I also did some other special projects that had duplicating negatives and enlarging black and white prints by hand. It was a great job, but not without its issues. I was overworked there and was burning out really fast. I had to keep asking for raises because I was the backbone of both the locations functioning properly, and the owner wouldn't even get the printing machine serviced or cleaned when it was supposed to. I was doing 4 people s jobs, and then on the weekends I would walk from center city around 18th and Market St. and go all the way down broad street til I hit South street, and then go to my other job and work till midnight. I had 18 hour days over the weekends and I wouldn't have changed it for the world. I was young, and it felt great when I could actually pay for my own bills, and was able to buy new sneakers whenever I wanted to, not to mention finish my back piece, which really did take a solid year or two to complete.

Two weeks of Kage being gone, and I had never heard from him. He never called me or wondered how I was doing. I wasn't a totally needy type of person when it comes to love and affection, in fact I usually hated it. But this was a bit too far to the other extreme. So after 2 weeks with no word, I considered myself to be single. Eventually he called me and I broke up with him on the phone. He begged and pleaded but I wouldn't give in. I wasn't looking for love when I met him, and so I was totally fine with being by myself. You see, there it is again. When you want things so bad, they don't come to you easily. One of the biggest lessons I have ever learned from living. When you're not looking for it, it will find you. As long as you are sure of what you want out of life, you will get it. But you can't be insecure about it. And you certainly can't be so greedy about it that you try to hunt it down before you're ready. It will find you. Have faith. That's how it was with Kage. And I only realized it a few years ago. I was meant to go to college for the sole purpose of meeting my husband. That's what God had planned for me.

Kage's friend ended up calling me later on and asked me to take him back. He agreed that what he did was stupid, but that he had no idea how to treat a girlfriend, and vowed to not let it happen again, and he did not. Oh if we only had cell phones.

By the end of 1998 I started feeling sick a lot. Kage was straight, and every time I smoked around him, he would make fun of me. I didn't want to quit smoking but I had started feeling so sick and had coughed up blood a few times, that I became very worried. I did cut back, but still seemed to have some sort of sickness. I didn't have health insurance, and the thought of ever going to the doctor or ER had never crossed my mind. Another month or two goes by and I have missed my period. I took a test and then it was confirmed that I was pregnant. I was only 19 years old. I had my whole life ahead of me and was just starting to actually enjoy my life when I was hit with this. I talked it over with Kage, not knowing what to do and he gave me the ultimate decision. He was actually on the other side of the country still on tour when we had to make such a huge life altering decision. I didn't know what to do and I had no one to turn to. I was alone and had no one. All I could do was revert back to my insecurities and the pain that I had endured as a child. I had vowed that I would never get married, and certainly never bring a child into this terrible disgusting world. Why would I make a child come into this world, only to endure pain in suffering? It seemed pretty selfish to me that anyone would do this to another human being. This world and everyone in it is suffering. Why bring in more children. Why repeat the cycle? I was even more worried about what my mom and grandma would say and do to me. I was 19 but I still felt like that 5 year old child waiting for the non stop mental abuse. I was so scared. I had run from that once, I didn't want to have to go back to it. So I made a choice.

I was not allowed to go there by myself, since it's an in and out procedure and it's very hard on the body mentally and physically. Kage offered to fly back home, but I said to just stay put and I invested in my friend to join me for support. It was only a few blocks away from my apartment, and so we walked there together with a jar filled with my piss for the doctors to test upon arrival. We went through security, as everyone had to do since this planned parenthood was often targeted by religious groups. And once in the building, I sat waiting patiently. Once my name was called they had me follow them into a room where they had my chart and took an ultrasound. They printed out a few pictures and attached them to the front of the folder. I had to then follow them into another room where they had me lay down and with my friend by my side, they stuck a long tube up my vagina. It was hooked to a pumping, sucking machine that had tubes leading into a very large container. And as they turned it on with the loud noises of the machine, I began to feel the most terrible pain I had ever felt in my whole life. It lasted for a really long time as it just sucked the life of an unborn innocent fetus out of my uterus. I screamed in pain as I held my friend's hand and squeezed with every ounce of life I had. This was all my fault and I am a terrible person for doing such a heinous act to another living soul. At first I was just glad it was over. I knew I was totally incapable of being a mother, especially a good one. My whole life was pain, and that's all I would have been able to show him. I know now in my heart that it was a little boy. He came to me during a reading by a medium only last year. I had no idea about what she was talking about until hours later. I had suppressed all memories of that child, and what terrible thing I did. But he came through and to me that was his way of forgiveness. I needed to forgive myself as I had spent so many years in depression and in guilt. I only did what I thought was the right decision. I always regretted it, and if you have regrets then you are not living. I had to learn from my mistakes, and it took me many years, but I finally learned. I am sorry for what I have done, but I don't regret it anymore. I never told my family what happened, and I had only ever shared it with 3 people. It was just one of those things people don't want to talk about. I ended up quitting smoking in a combination of whatever sickness I had which people had told me was associated with the Newports I had chain smoked, and in combination with the pregnancy. I replaced the cigarettes with candy and food and ended up gaining a good 10-15 pounds after that. It just became a part of the depression that I was in, and had always suffered from since I was young. Only this was like the next level. It was really hard to go through but without having Kage there, I know that my life would have been totally different. I know without a doubt that I would be living on the streets. Two months later he proposed.

11

Trauma Bonding Love

As a result of my parents not showing me love or attention, I didn't know or learn how to give it. It was difficult for her to love herself, and even more difficult for her to show it towards me. The only way I got attention was by acting out, but then that subsided as well. It didnt matter what I did for attention or love, the only way I got it was through sex and men. Once I was married though and things got normal, we both got complacent. Showing love towards him was me doing his laundry. His way of showing love to me was supplying a place to live and food. It was survival and what we had both reciprocated as love and affection towards each other. I am not saying this as a bad thing. It worked for a very long time. I just didn't know that I was living in that state, my body still in full panic and trauma, fight, flight or freeze, responses. My relationship and my environment reflected these things to me only I wasn't aware enough at the time to see it for myself. In fact from the outside perspective it looked like we were the perfect couple, living the perfect lives that everyone strived for and were jealous of.

All I have wanted was for someone to take care of me and to feel safe. He was able to provide that for me. I always felt safe around him, his presence was grounding and he always made me laugh. His sense of humor was what attracted me the most to him. He still makes me laugh to this day.

After the abortion, and the proposal I had decided that things needed to go real slow. I had always told myself that I would live my life alone, and just be happy with being alone. After all, I knew I could count on myself. But meeting Kage had changed all that, and I really didn't want to mess it up. So I thought a long engagement would at least make up for the fact that we had only been dating for a few months before had moved in with each other, and only a few months after that had we gotten engaged.

We were engaged for 2 years before we finally got married. We had bought our first house in south philly 10th and Dickinson street which really laid the groundwork for what it has been turned into today, a highly sought after hipster area with trendy bars and restaurants. I should have known that getting married wouldn't change anything. But I was naive. We honeymooned in Hawaii, and it was beautiful of course, but our first night was hardly what you would expect as a newly married couple. I had prepared for the night, with the help of my friends from my bridal shower with lots of outfits and what not. We sat in the hotel the first night as he went to grab a soda from the vending machine. I took the opportunity to have time by myself to get dressed up in the cute outfit I had gotten to surprise him with and wait for him to come back to the room to surprise him. As he walks in the room, I surprise him and could not have been more disappointed and let down than if I had tried. He was totally not interested in me at all, and the fight ended with him throwing his wedding ring at me. We ended up making up because I don't like having confrontations and just kept stuffing things deep down inside. I felt rejected by my own husband and I didnt want to feel that way or put myself in that predicament again. So I kept on hiding and stuffing parts of myself down into the dark.

By the time we had decided to try to have kids was the time that I thought Karma really was coming back around. I had been off birth control for a long time, yet I was unable to get pregnant. I felt then that I just didn't deserve to be a mother since I had an opportunity to be one before which I had aborted. I didn't deserve to have that type of love in my life. It really takes a toll on a woman when you are trying to get pregnant and it doesn't come naturally or easily. It makes you feel like a failure, like it's your fault. It made me feel hopeless and like all blame was placed upon me. This is something not enough women talk about either. It goes straight into action, go do this, go do that to fix the problem, instead of letting us *feel*. Talk about the feelings of what we are going through, not just giving us answers of how to perform a task that needs to be completed.

And after almost a full year of trying, I had finally given up on it. I ended up getting pregnant with my daughter immediately after that.

I was so scared to be a mother. I didn't know what on earth I was doing. I watched the baby shows on TV and thought ok, it can't be that hard, giving birth, being a mother. I certainly knew what *not* to do. I was extremely well versed in that category after all I had spent the first 20 years of my life learning what not to do to my child by experiencing it first hand.

I had spent years trying to accomplish a personal goal and get into a career I wanted since I was a teenager, being a tattoo artist. It was so difficult trying to get into a career that had no room for women. It was a completely different lifestyle back then in the late 90's then it is today. There were zero woman artists to look up to. We only had magazines as a source of inspiration or local shops. There was no social media. I worked my ass off begging, learning on my own, and paying people to teach me. I worked at a few shops until eventually finding a place to stay on South Street that I had worked at for 5 years before getting pregnant.

The hours were difficult for me to wrap my head around in order to be a mother. I worked from noon till around midnight, sometimes later if it was the weekend and during the summer. It was clear that I needed to leave my job and stay home with our daughter so my husband could focus on his career and I stayed at home instead of hiring childcare.

As a result of all the trauma I had suffered I was terrified to even think about leaving my child with anyone that wasn't me. I wouldn't ever be able to forgive myself if anything remotely traumatic happened to my own daughter. I worked at the shop up until I couldn't physically bend over anymore to tattoo. I had about a month between the time I left my job as a tattoos artist until our daughter was born.

Up until our daughter was born we had always split everything equally for our living expenses. Even though I wanted to be taken care of and have a stable environment, it was extremely difficult for me to let someone else provide for me, or offer me anything I didn't feel like I deserved. I was so proud of the accomplishment of becoming a tattoo artist that it hurt me for a long time that I had felt like I had given up on myself and being artistic. It felt like a part of me died. A part of my identity. The part of me that reached an almost impossible goal and the part of me that had always relied on myself. I gave it up to become a mother, and to offer my life to someone else. My daughter and my husband. At this time Kage provided financial stability and security for not only myself but our little family we had finally created together. The other things I was looking for as a result of the childhood I had grown up in.

Being a mother was difficult for me in the beginning. I had no one to turn to or ask for help or for advice from. I was alone. My mother was not in my life and I had been the only one out of my friend group in Philly to have kids. I swear I didn't sleep for the first 3 months postpartum. I was so depressed and confused. When I think about it now as I look back all I remember is how much I cried, how much I laid there on the couch while she lay in a carrier that swung and how all I wanted was for someone, anyone to help me.

After three months I started to get into the groove of things. I stopped listening to the pediatrician because he kept telling me that I had to wake her up to feed her. What a ridiculous concept. This is the advice I listened to and many others, and it was terrible. I realized that if she was hungry she would wake up! Wow, what on earth are they teaching doctors in medical school? A baby has the ability to tell you if it's hungry. It's like one of the things they can do. I am still in shock at how much our medical communities are failing us. It has been a constant catalyst for me though to get me to where I am today. So I am thankful for it in my life, but how much havoc has it already caused for others? (Small rant over) I finally started to learn to listen and be attuned to her and not what others told me. It was beautiful to witness her cooes and her movements. It was like I was reading her mind without doing anything. We got into a grove and all of a sudden it's a few years later and we had moved across the bridge to New Jersey for a better family experience.

12 |

Victimhood

The codependency grew over the years, especially because I started feeling helpless and stuck. I think the only reason we lasted so long was because of his job. He traveled for a living, he spent more time away then he did at home and that meant we barely saw each other. It worked out perfectly. Although we were very unaware of it at the time, since we weren't around each other, we didn't have to be shown the things in which we really needed to work on, both as individuals and as a couple in a partnership. I took care of my job as a stay at home mother and he did his job of being a provider. And so it went on.

Having my son 3 and a half years later was another big challenge. After a few months we found out that I had placenta previa. The doctor told me I had to be mostly bed ridden during my pregnancy with the hopes that it would eventually correct itself. For months, as if I could feel even more alone, I was then told I couldnt be active either. Keeping a toddler close to home and trying not to be active was difficult. Not interacting with others sent me into another depression, in addition to being worried about my son having issues with the pregnancy.

Most of the rest of the pregnancy was a blur. I remember the day I went into labor, that will stick with me until another time when I change that story. My son had issues from the day he was born and throughout his infancy that became even more of a catalyst for me to question things within the medical system even more. For a long time Kage really denied our son had any issues. He just wouldn't face the fact that his only son was different. It took him many years I think to finally see that our son deserves his love and attention too. But I often played the victim when he was young. Telling myself it was my fault he was autistic. All I did was complain and cry. Why me why me?

Once I let go of being a victim, I started working hard to help him be the best person he can be. And he really is the best. He is the absolute light of my life and I wouldn't have it any other way. Instead of saying "why me" I say "thank you God" I often hear other moms with ASD kids whine and complain about how hard life is with them. But they are looking at the wrong end of it. Yes, it is hard but I believe that God gives us exactly what we can handle. We just have a choice to make whether we follow our path, or complain about it. My life has been enriched in so many ways by having him and I would never change it for anything in this world.

He was diagnosed with Autism late at 5 and 1/2 Years old. Part of the reason was because his father and I were both in denial, the other reasons are because once we decided to have him checked out for a diagnosis in New Jersey we became one of many many people on a 2 year waiting list. Two years to see doctors to tell us if he can be labeled and thrown into a box. NJ has the highest rate of children on the Autism spectrum, at the time I had looked it up, and so that I am sure is the reason for the waiting list. This also should bring some concerns as to why....why NJ..? They also have the highest amount of required vaccinations. They also house a lot of major pharmaceutical manufacturers. Not to mention other major corporations spewing chemicals into the air and waters. I digress.

We were just a few months from our appointment when we had to move out of the state of NJ and into NY. It was a trying time. Once settled into our new house I found the resources and we then became one family among others that were on only a 6-8 month waiting list. Once his appointment came, as a family we all went to the appointment to support him. He had to take multiple tests for different areas of development, After spending the entire day there they left us with "Thomas doesn't fit into a typical mold."

I knew this already because of how drastically different he was since we started the journey of trying to get a diagnosis when he was between the ages of 2 and 3. Which was already very late because of our denial. The group of doctors and therapists decided to watch him in school the following week. Once they came together and made a decision, I got the call. He was diagnosed as being on the spectrum of Autism. By the time this had come it really didn't even matter to me anymore. I knew he was different and that something had happened to him when he was 3 months old that had changed him. The only thing the diagnosis did for us was help to get him more support in his classroom setting. This was a huge help to him, and to us. I am thankful for the diagnosis but know that he no longer fits into that mold in any way shape or form if he were to be evaluated today.

As I write this today he is 11 years old and in the 5th grade. If you met him outside of school you would have no idea he is anywhere on the spectrum. There are MANY things I contribute to this but what I want to talk about is the start of when it all began to change. For us it all started with changing our pediatrician. Thomas was about 2-3 years old at this time. I was sick of the office we were going to. They didn't care, they were judgemental, and I am convinced they did more damage than anything. I was watching tv one day and saw a celebrity pediatrician on a talk show. I was intrigued so I looked him up and found his office that he had just opened up. I was so excited that I was able to get an appointment and totally ignored that the office was 2 1/2 hours away from our house. YES, I drove 5 hours (2.5 hours one way) with my kids every time they went to the office. I was that desperate for a pediatrician that actually *cared* about children.

"The Whole Child Center" was green, environmentally friendly, and the office was so clean and inviting. The staff was so nice and I was shocked that Doctor Rosen spent more than an hour with us in the room talking about what was going on with my child. When does that happen in our medical communities, ever? It doesn't. Just having someone taking the time to listen to me made a drastic difference in our lives. Dr. Rosen is proof that good people exist in the medical world. He talked about a supplement that seemed to work for his patients with great results so I was willing to give it a try, even with the hefty price tag. It was a liquid capsule and so I would prick it with a pin and put it in Thomas's drinks everyday. He never even noticed. Within a few weeks I started to notice how different he was, he was more engaging, and though there was still no eye contact, he seemed a little more balanced. I kept giving him the supplements because it was an improvement, and any improvement is big for a child with Autism. This supplement changed Thomas for the better. It gave him a little spark. It was called "Speak" and that's exactly what it ended up doing for him. In combination and support from his therapists and teachers Thomas began to speak. Just a few words but over the next year he added more and more and more.

I started doing research on diet because a friend had told me that they started giving their child "Green Machine" and saw great results. I quickly started him on the green juice every morning and then started switching him over to a gluten/dairy free and a metal detoxing diet. Of course, he improved. Keeping bread off his plate was a challenge and so I tried to limit it as much as I could and it was better than what he used to eat. Changing diets can be extremely challenging and so some of the time as long as he ate something healthy I was happy. The progress was slow which is why we don't even think about it today when we look at him. But that is the thing, we forgot what he used to be like! He is that different today then compared to when he was little.

When he was 8 months old through the age of 5, he was nonverbal and very violent. He would hurt himself by throwing his head back and arching his back to the point that he had bruises and carpet burns all over his poor sweet head. Not to mention how many times I got hurt in the process by being in the way. He just had no other way to communicate and so that's how the violence would be triggered.

I fed him strawberries everyday because it was the only fruit he would eat on his own, and would put cilantro in his smoothies. I started making vegetable and fruit smoothies with almond, soy or coconut milk. Adding as many ingredients that I could because he was, as most Autistic kids are, extremely picky about food. Luckily I never had to worry as long as it had a taste that was sweet in the end.

The other thing I want to stress besides diet,vitamins, supplements and therapies, is the work that the parents do. In my case it was pretty much just me, but it is most important for the mother to do the work. Not on just a physical level, but on a more emotional, subtle level. The mother has got to change her mindset about a diagnosis. The victim state only fuels it.

As soon as I stopped looking at him as a punishment and like I was a victim of something terrible, our whole lives changed again. He had less anger...and obviously it started with me. I looked at him as a gift and it had sparked something within me. I started to work on myself at that moment. I started with yoga and then went to therapy and well more and more healing happened. The deeper I went into my own healing, the better I got mentally, and the better he got mentally as well.

The moment you start working on yourself on a deeper level then it automatically reflects downwards into our children. I am still changing today and can't wait to see how it affects my children. It still happens. In fact, it also goes backwards generationally. It's not as profound as going down generation wise but it still does something positive. As parents, and particularly as a mother, we have a responsibility. We can change our DNA, our genetic makeup and reverse the harm that toxins create in our bodies. My son is living proof.

We can help our children to heal by healing ourselves. And never, ever stop.

I had changed alot since I was young, and had changed even more since I was a young angry teenager full of hatred for the world. I still have many

many layers to shed, and still have a few left as I write this now but I know I am much closer to being a better person than I was yesterday. Each thing we go through can easily shape us as a human being. Each traumatic event gets etched out into our brain and gets stored energetically within our body.

For me, trying to find ways of making connections to things I know harm my true potential has been a hard path, but one that has been needed in order to help me heal. I have been through so much in my life that it has been a really difficult thing to have to face. When my husband met me, I was afraid to be in cars, I was afraid of leaving the house, as a borderline agoraphobic, and I refused to answer the phone because I had so much anxiety. I wouldn't be able to go anywhere by myself. All of these things and more have been a direct result of the trauma that I have been through. It happened and it has been my job, and my job only to face it and to overcome it. I wasn't going to make excuses anymore. I had to stop blaming others, blaming my parents and circumstances. I was the one in charge of my own life and I had to do something about it.

Having my daughter really did help in some of my healing, as I went in and out of depression that seemed to rotate around me like a clock. Always around 3 months in and 3 months out of it. When I was in depression, I was really in it. Unable to move, unable to leave the house, unable to get out of bed and when I did, it was to only move to the couch. Having my daughter really helped me get through it, as she was always such a beautiful light in my life. She helped me find the little spark inside myself, and she probably will never know how much she helped me without even trying. Having my son was a different story and ultimately a huge lesson from God. I do believe God gives us exactly what we need, and just what we are able to handle.

My son taught me a huge lesson, and that was patience. I could go on and on about the horrors I had to endure with him, while I tried to live day by day in a constant state of survival. But it got to a point, where I was unable to go out in public with him anymore. The first few years he would bang his head on the floor because it was his only way of communicating his frustrations. If he wasn't in a stroller, he would run away, and for a boy who was full on walking by 8 months he sure was fast. We had ended up becoming recluses and hardly ever left our house. I ordered all my groceries online and was able to drive my minivan to the grocery store and pick them up. I had a routine and it was the only way I was able to survive. I had no family or friends to help me at this point, as when my son was born, after we had already moved to a better area out of the city, all our friends pretty much stopped visiting. My son was difficult to be around, and so I never blamed my friends for not stopping over as much anymore. None of them had kids and so it was a little too much for them to endure when they really just wanted to have fun.

Eventually we started receiving services for my son at the house. We started focusing on speech language as a way to communicate and it slowly stopped him from physical violence to himself and others. He really needed a lot of help and he was way behind in every aspect. Thankfully he was getting better every day with a changed diet and with therapy.

In the midst of this my best friend kept telling me I needed to try yoga. I often made fun of her and thought yoga was for old people. We had gone on vacation once together with our families and in the early morning hours I watched her in the backyard doing yoga. I just giggled at her while peering out the window, and went on assuming it was lame. Isn't it just something people did laying on the floor and moving a leg here or there? That seemed really boring to me, and so I always declined. I also didn't understand why she would drive an hour and a half for just a yoga class that was down the street from me. I eventually was in so much stress that when my friend had told me to go to yoga again for the third time in one week, I finally caved. I knew I needed to try something. My life was in shambles, including my marriage, and my husband's business. There wasn't anything in my life that was going well, and I needed something. I didn't care what it was, I needed to try something to get my life back on track.

The first Ashtanga Mysore Yoga class I attended, I just sat in the back and watched. I was too scared to agree to jump into it head first without even knowing what I was in for. It's part of my need for constant control. I would only go with my friend Danielle, because of my shyness and anxiety level which was through the roof whenever I left my house. She picked me up and I sat in the back of the mysore room and just watched the students as they seemed to flow and breathe without any thought or care in the world. I was in complete awe of them, and I wanted to do what they were doing. Little did I know they had all been practicing for many many years, that's why they made it look so easy. I was in for a rude awakening.

The next day I came back with Dana and started my first class learning what a Sun Salutation was. I have to give a lot of credit to my teacher, Shelly, because I know now that when I walked into that room, I was a totally lost, broken soul. Inside and out. She would show me what to do, and in the very next moment, I couldn't remember what to do. I couldn't touch my toes. I had never done a physical activity in my life, ever. And by the time I showed up here in my early thirties, I was so stiff and it was unbelievably hard for me to do any of it. I think I was there for maybe half an hour, and I was fully drenched in sweat from head to toe. It was a heated room to 85 but on top of that, I was so insecure that I had a sports bra on, 2 tank tops (one tight and one loose) and then a shirt on top of all that. I usually kept on my sweatshirt until I was just so hot I couldn't take it anymore. I even wore baggy yoga pants because I hated wearing anything tight. It scared me. It made me think I was objectifying myself to potential rapists. Subconsciously, of course. I wore baggy clothes, pants and huge shirts to hide any part of my female figure and yoga was no exception.

The teacher told me I had to commit to 8 weeks and made me pay in advance, which seemed like no problem until the first class. I didn't know how I was going to get through all the rest of the 8 weeks. It was so difficult, I didn't think I would ever be able to learn anything. Not only did I have such problems doing the actual physical activity, but

I had an even harder time memorizing the sequence. A part of what's unique about this form of yoga is the memorization of the set sequence. I had never done any yoga before this so I didn't know any different at the time. But it was hard.

Giving up never seemed an option for me since I had already paid for my 8 weeks and I was a stingy mother of two. I couldn't think of wasting a single penny, even if we were doing well financially. It's in my blood to be cheap. It took me the full 8 weeks to learn that sun salutation which to most other practitioners would sound like a joke. I didn't know it was odd, or a long time to be learning one thing as my teacher had never indicated anything to me about how I was doing. We are all different and no one is better or worse than the other. For one person it may take one class to learn, for me it took longer. By the end of the 8 weeks I was hooked. I had gone from not being able to remember or do anything before I had started, and by the end I felt like I had actually accomplished something. Even if it was only Sun Salutations. In that short time, I had understood that Ashtanga yoga was very powerful. I signed up for the next month and the next month and I was hooked. When the teacher said I could start practicing everyday, I spent 3 days a week at the studio and the other days practicing at home. I tried my hardest and never gave up.

One day on the mat at the studio, I seemed to be having a very difficult time at home with what was going on with my family and it showed up on the mat. I stood there not being able to remember what standing pose came next. I stared at the wall, at my feet until a sense of emotions, sadness and then embarrassment overcame me. I started balling my eyes out. I then removed myself to sit in the back of the room where the cubbies were. Sitting in a chair, I cried my eyes out not realizing what was even wrong. I tried to compose myself but the thought that I had no idea what I was supposed to do made me even more upset. Eventually my friend came to sit with me to make sure I was ok. She had assured me that everyone was crying in the mysore room and made me feel like I wasn't alone. If she wasn't there, my fight or flight reflexes would have set in, as they often did and I would have just walked out and never came back. But she made me feel safe, and made me feel like it was ok to cry and let it out, and so I did. This was the first time I cried during yoga, but it certainly wasn't the last.

She went back to practice as I calmed myself down. I sat for another 5 minutes and still couldn't remember what pose to do. I finally snuck a peak of the David Swenson book that lay on the table which I am sure was obvious since the room was silent except for the sound of the breath. Now that I knew what came next, I made my way back to my mat and continued practicing. Even though I had to look at a book to remember, I had learned a huge lesson that day. I knew that yoga was working and it started my way to truly healing from the inside out. Everything in my life has come to surface through yoga, and it's not always pretty. In fact, it's hardly ever been pretty for me. But that day I knew, I was in this practice for life. It was my destiny and I never looked back except as a reminder as to just how far I have come since then.

Every single thing that happened to me on the mat was a reflection of my life off the mat and vice versa. Yoga has a way of making you confront things you are too scared to. It also teaches you that with hard work, you were able to confront them, head on and overcome them. You had the power to work through your crap. The power of Ashtanga yoga was and is amazing. It is not something that is easily explained in words even. It's an experience. It taught me that even though I was damaged goods, I was still worthy of life. It taught me that despite my very slow progress, I was still progressing. It taught me to be compassionate to myself and other people. It taught me how to love myself, and most importantly it taught me how to love. Now it's not an easy process, and it has been a long one but I put up the fight, stuck with it and I am finally able to say that I have found myself and I have found love. Love for myself.

My daughter taught me that there were more important things to life than having self pity and playing a victim. She taught me that being a child can be fun and let me have a childhood I had always wanted through the eyes of her. I was always planning every single day for us to live to its purest and highest potential. We went to the zoo once a week, to the children's museum once a week, to the outdoor parks every single week. Our weekly rituals shaped each other and taught us both a lot. The Philadelphia Zoo created my daughter's passion for animals. The Please Touch Museum while it was in its original building, shaped my love for kids of all ages. The playgrounds made me feel like a child, and the child that I should have been able to be. I was able to have a full life, I just ended up being a kid later on. And I wouldn't change it for anything.

I was always the only parent playing with their child. I swung on the swings with her, I went down the slides with her, I tried my best to play on the monkey bars. I interacted with every fake grocery store, pretending to buy ingredients to bake fake pies. I often wondered, especially while we were at the playgrounds, what is more important to these other parents than to interact with your own kids? Of course I didn't know how they acted at home. I only saw little slivers of their lives for a few hours a week. I just never understood why I was the only one acting like a child. I was really good at being a kid. I was the kid I had always felt was inside of me that wasn't able to be let out until then.

My son taught me patience. Boy did he ever. Any parent of a child with a disability can understand just what that means. It's hard enough raising kids without disabilities, but adding on top of it is another hardship and you're in a world of crap that is hard for anyone else to understand. I try joining groups of other parents of Autistic kids, but all I hear over and over again is them playing the victims. It's exactly what it was like when I went to an AA meeting a couple years ago when I was struggling with alcohol. A friend had brought me to one with all women and I sat there for an hour while listening to these people's terrible stories of alcohol abuse. Of course I can't repeat anything I had heard, but the stories were terrible. Every time another person would speak, it had nothing to do with alcohol at all. I could hear their stories, and I could tell where in their lives they went wrong and wanted to shake them and say, just fix it. Just stop. Just stop playing the victim. And then I realized I had found my way back to the victim within myself. I was judging them for something I couldn't see within myself. Why does my son have autism? Why me? Why why why? I was petrified and scared as to what life was going to be like for him, for me, for us.

I realized at that one AA meeting, that I just had to change and so I did. I stopped drinking for about 6 months. We had ended up moving away to another state in Central NY which may as well be in the middle of nowhere. I had lost my Ashtanga studio, and no longer had a teacher. I lasted a few months without her, practicing everyday, but then I started to feel stuck as I had no one to tell me what to do anymore. The brutal winter was starting and I once again fell back into depression, and along with it came the end of practicing yoga, and then the drinking started again. When I stopped practicing yoga, which was a 6 day a week practice, I started having physical withdrawals. There is actually a name for it, I had to look it up because it was so painful. Just as the soreness of the muscles had been created while I was using and making them, I had the same, if not worse soreness from stopping the use of them. Slowly, week by week it was a different group of muscles as if my body was unlearning each and every pose, one by one. It in turn made me even go deeper into my depression.

Only this time it didn't stick around. I had learned so many tools along my journey, that I was able to get myself out of it quicker. I had stopped practicing for about 2 months when I had then decided that I had to do something about it, and that I could never leave Ashtanga yoga out of my life again, for any reason. The alcohol though kept creeping in and out of my life a little bit longer.

For some reason conventional treatments did not have the same effect on me as it did most other people. I think it was because I was just too intune with the universe and I was starting to see my own strength. I had spent a year in and out of drinking binges, though I was never in danger of hurting anyone but myself. I only drank at home by myself, and I would start drinking while the kids were still in school. I never got drunk, as I would only have enough to feel a nice buzz and then was able to just be with myself in my depression. Being an adult, no family around and living in a new state with only a few friends who have families of their own made me feel alone again. The worse I got mentally, the worse I ended up getting physically. My relationship with my husband was so terrible and toxic that we barely even talked to each other. I just wanted the relationship to end. I wanted everything to end. I felt defeated. My body was starting to tell me things that I was ignoring mentally, emotionally and spiritually. It was trying to get my attention and I was using a lot of energy ignoring it.

I started having pain in my lower back that I was ignoring. Praying that ignoring it would make it go away. Just like my life, and my husband.

At one point later down the line when I had gone to my first talk therapy session by myself to work on my own problems, not marriage stuff, I had found myself in a really surprising predicament. I learned through talk therapy that as a result of my trauma, I am what is known as a slow processor. Meaning I take a long time, longer than the average person, to process things in my brain. I had been doing so much work on myself through Ashtanga Yoga and I knew I was really close to having a breakthrough. I was learning so much about myself and about how my body has stored my trauma that I wanted to work at it from every angle. I had been writing, journaling since I went to rehab as a pointer from the social worker, but it just wasn't enough to get to the root of it all. I decided I was finally ready to go see a therapist and to talk more deeply about it. It was a really hard decision because I had been called a liar by my mother every time I had seen one growing up. If anyone had believed me instead of her, she would have ended up in jail, and rightly so. This time I was ready for someone to hear my side of things and to start speaking my truth.

13

Taking Matters Into My Own Hands

I walked into the therapist's office and in the first half hour I got straight to the point. I was molested repeatedly when I was 5, I was physically and mentally abused, neglected and was also raped by a friend as a teenager, and then raped again by someone else at a party. I know this is why I act the way I act in certain situations. I want to know how I can stop reacting to people, stop being afraid of everyone, everything and how I can become a normal person.

I must have shocked her because it took her a minute to figure out what to say to me. Her response was one that I will never forget, and totally did not expect.

"These are things that we work through in therapy. We usually take months and months to get to the point where you are now. Since you are already at this point, I am sorry, but there is nothing I can help you further with."

I was completely shocked and devastated. What she said and what I had heard were different things. I heard, translated through my foggy mind, that I was too far gone and can't be helped. My victim mentality heard that I was worthless, and not someone that was deserving of help in any way.

You're a therapist to help people with trauma and what I had heard was that I wasn't able to be saved? Of course, that is not what she was saying. What she was actually saying was that I had done a lot of work on myself and that I had basically skipped that step of learning through a therapist about where these things came from. It took me a long time to get to that conclusion. I resent her for a while in between learning about the cloudiness within my own mind's perception and the reality of things.

She gave me a few yoga therapists that she thought would be able to help me, which never panned out. I was only dedicated to the Ashtanga yoga method, and when the teachers didn't write me back, or I didn't get a good vibe from that path, I let it be and moved on. The therapist did give me the name of a book to read and so I ordered it right away. I tried reading it, but the words were so difficult for me to understand. I quickly got lost in just trying to translate the thing into layman's terms. Eventually I just bought the audio version of it, and I had earbuds in my ears nonstop for days and days.

That book changed my life. It was a huge pivotal moment in my healing. I mentioned earlier, it was called *The Body Keeps The Score* by Bessel van der Kolk. My mind was blown after every chapter. I had made so many connections that seemed unreal, only to be validated through the stories and research of this man's life work. It was amazing to me that mental health has not been talked enough about in our culture. We have all the answers, this doctor has so many options for treatment yet so many millions of people are suffering. I wish I could just add his whole book to this book, as it has had such an impact on me, but I will leave that up to you to go find on your own path.

This book showed me that I seemed to be on the right path, and I was so excited for the future. I started realizing the connections between the past and present and it helped me to create new patterns. It was really, really hard and soon my husband and I were both in counseling together and separate. It was really hard work, but we both put the effort in. We had to figure out something because once I had gone away to a yoga intensive training I came back and decided I wanted to leave him. Yoga was a big catalyst for change within me. It was almost to blame for the struggles we were having, although we know that not really true, it seemed to be from the outsiders perspective especially his.

I had spent months in so much physical pain, that I had started realizing that besides having a serious problem with my back, it felt that it went deeper than just my spine. I had spent weeks not even able to walk without physical pain, and had to figure out a way to heal myself because my doctors' appointments were all weeks away from the MRI scan I had just had. I had to wait months before a doctor could look at the MRI results and prescribe me anything, physical therapy or other. I couldn't just sit there and waste away. I had to do something about it. I had to heal myself. Again.

I started researching my pain symptoms online, I kept stepping on my mat every day and then I started a journal. A sort of pain journal if you will. I kept doing my practice and if certain things hurt, or made me feel worse I would keep track of it and start editing it out of my practice. Eventually I was only doing sun salutations because my back became so severe. But I still made it to the mat. Don't get me wrong, there were a few days where I made it to the mat and literally just collapsed and balled my eyes out or sat there and wrote in a journal. My intentions were still there. I still made it to the mat, everyday.

I ended up finding some poses that felt good for my back, and decided that what I was really supposed to do was to be moving forward in the practice, instead of going backwards. As soon as I came to that realization I started doing more backbending postures and my back started healing. It was a really slow process, I took it day by day but I was improving. While I had gone to that yoga intensive I had learned a lot about the spine and the energetic locks in the body. I had still been modifying poses and later when we had a discussion with the teachers, I had asked specifically if he could talk to me about the yogic knots of the spine that he had briefly mentioned earlier.

He told me that I needed to stop thinking and to just breathe. It sounds very easy, but is in fact extremely difficult. Especially for me, an overthinker. The next day while we were practicing my back started hurting in the poses it usually did. I stopped for a moment and said to myself, just breathe. Just breathe. Just breathe. And the pain literally left my body. A few poses later and I started talking in my head. Wow it doesn't hurt anymore. Holy crap it doesn't hurt. And then on cue, it started hurting..only it was the other side this time. The side that wasn't injured. I laughed and said, I know what you're doing to me. And I am not going to give in. It doesn't hurt. It doesn't hurt. Just breathe. And with that the pain went away. It was gone until I had arrived back home. Ashtanga yoga has a way of showing you exactly what you need to work on, only in a subtle way.

Upon my arrival back home my husband ignored me as if I had never left. The next day we started arguing and in the middle of the argument, sharp pains in my lower back. This pain I was feeling wasn't an injury. It was energetic and I had finally made that connection. I had gone to the doctors already by this time. I had my MRI examined and saw the specialists. I had a bulging disc, but it had been 6 months since the original incident of being unable to walk and by then it was already healed through the work I had been doing on my own through yoga. So why was I still feeling pain during, what seemed to be random, acts of living life? Because I couldn't let it go. I made it a part of my story, and so it just lingered around me. I was attached to the pain and being in a state of victimhood that I was unable to see. I had the power to make it go away and yet I wasn't able to. Once I had made the connection, I had spent a whole month seperated from my husband. Living with friends on the weekends, and alternating being at home with the kids. The kids never realized what was happening. Which was for the better. I had learned and grown as a person, and so I wasn't the person my husband married 17 years ago. I was a better version of myself and he didn't like it. He got from me what he needed because of his traumas. We were in a cycle of living until I had decided to change. If he wanted to be with me, then he needed to make an effort to change as well, and so he finally made the decision to change as well.

I stopped making myself a victim of back pain. Of pain in a terrible relationship and I changed it. We changed it together. It has been a year since that happened and we have never been in a better spot than we are right now. We still have our problems of course, and I still continue to work on myself. In fact, that's what has made me write all this stuff down. After 3 and ½ years of doing yoga by myself, I learned that I was my own teacher. I was able to learn and grow on my own when I had thought I had always needed someone else to teach me. Just when I had let go of needing and wanting a teacher, one had appeared before me. I had found my next yoga teacher, but he is more than just that one word. And of course, I had found him by mistake, when I wasn't even looking for a teacher. Which of course means it was totally not a coincidence and happened at exactly the time it was supposed to happen. Just have faith and keep your eyes open. The universe works for you, you just have to listen, be open, and just have trust and patience. Just believe.

The year 2016 was gearing me towards the meeting with that teacher and showing me what my true purpose in life was, to help others. Since I was a little girl, I knew I would be a teacher. I just never thought it would actually happen. Even last year I had wondered what I would teach. Should I teach people how to crochet, or would I teach people how to run a successful internet business? It wasn't until this year that I realized I was meant to be exactly what I already was, a yoga teacher and so much more. I had been teaching yoga for over 2 years by that point and I had never looked at it the same as other professions. Because I didn't do it to make money, I did it because I have to. Like a contract I signed before being born on this planet. The universe guided me here, and I just went with it. It had never occured to me until recently that I was already on the path that was meant for me. Exactly the way it was supposed to be.

Last year I had so much turmoil in my life but it had prepared me for today. The last 38 years I have been working through all my crap. It was the hardest thing I had ever done and really painful to the point where I thought I was crazy, and maybe I was, but I didn't know if I would come out of it alive. But I had made it through to the other side and this side is much better. I had to go through that pain in order to be able to be here now. Right now. I have never been more happy in my life, and so thankful to have a life. The pain I went through taught me how to be a better parent, a better friend, a better person, and a better teacher.

One of my therapy sessions had been an hour long discussion on how I was unable to receive gifts. It made me physically cave in, and very uncomfortable. As we worked on the source of where it came from, the therapist had me do an exercise which was to watch how other people reacted when they had been given a gift. I had to relearn how to accept a gift. It was a hard task, which I had improved upon, but it wasn't until later on when I understood the reason for the exercise which helped me learn what love was supposed to look like, or feel like.

I had started to be shown by the universe what love looks and feels like, what the most important thing in life is. The only thing you take with you when you are no longer flesh and blood. Love, it's all love. Working on making myself a better person, and yoga has shown me that. The most important thing I had learned during the Ashtanga Yoga Confluence had nothing to do with poses or yoga at all. It was a life lesson and boy was it beautiful. There were two teachers there, Eddie Stern and his wife Jocelyn. Just seeing them together made me feel loved and I wasn't even near them. I saw the meaning of love in their eyes and at that moment, I had realized what love looked like, and what love felt like. I felt their love, it filled the room, it filled their hearts. It filled my heart and it was awe inspiring. From that moment on I started seeing love everywhere. I started feeling love, I started being loved, and I started giving love. Unconditional love. Once you find love, the world changes. You see love in everyone and in everything.

I loved my husband, I loved my mother, I loved my father, I loved my step father, and I loved my sister. We may not have a perfect relationship, or in the case of my sister, have any relationship at all, but I still love them. That will never change.

2

Breaking The Cycles Of The Past

14

Yoga Studio

I had met my next yoga teacher, though he was in a different state, it gave me the energy to keep moving forward. I had been having conversations with him about how to start my own community where I was located in Central New York because there were none dedicated to the practice of Ashtanga yoga. He had given me advice from afar and I had moved my energy towards making that happen. I was working at the local yoga studio that I had taken my 200 hour teacher training certification with but was limited to one class per week on the studio schedule. I wanted to have a dedicated Mysore program where we were open early hours and had a class on the schedule 6 days a week. The owner of the studio was not willing to offer it despite my begging and pleading and even offering to not be paid unless there were enough students after expenses. I was frustrated but kept looking. I went to all the local studios, there were few but I ended up adding another weekly class to my teaching schedule even though I didn't find what I was looking for.

I had taught this way for a while until I eventually had found a place that would let me teach there. It was a dance studio, instead of a yoga studio and I had started with only offering the Mysore program there a few days a week. Eventually, we had a few more students and after a few months I had found an even better fit for a space, my own. I ended up moving into my own dedicated space for Ashtanga Yoga.

Having my own studio space felt like such an accomplishment. It had felt like it was difficult to get there but when I look back I wasn't really ready to do it until the space showed up to me. It came to me, I wasn't looking for it. I had been walking down the street and there was a sign, clear as day on the sidewalk. "Space for Rent." I called the number and moved into it immediately. Divine timing is such an important concept. Even if we want something so bad and get frustrated that things don't go our way, we must ask if the timing is right. If its not, we must trust the universe that it will happen when it's meant to, as long as we keep trying and are open to it instead of trying to force it with control.

The yoga studio taught me a lot of things, most of all, it taught me about energy and about the students reflecting back to me things that I was not able to see on my own. It taught me that I needed to show up for myself not only for my own life but for all of the people around me as well. The more I showed up for myself on the mat the more others around me took accountability for their own life. When I put energy into myself I had energy for my children and it gave me the capacity to see and understand how other people were showing up in their own lives and their jobs and in their families.

Having a studio and my own Mysore program made me show up to the studio every morning. I would get there at 5 AM so I could do my own practice and be finished by the time the students came there around 7:30 AM. Some mornings were easier than others most especially the ones when the weather was cooperative. During the winter months it would not be guaranteed that I would have heat in the studio or electricity for that matter. It's an interesting dynamic that I had to work myself around dealing with the landlord and also with the caretaker of the property. I grinned and beared it because I wanted to have this studio for myself, for my livelihood and to keep me in line. It also made me feel accomplished and I was able to create and establish a community with people that were like minded. We had potlucks where people would interact with each other, bring nice healthy food to share with each other and we learned a lot about the people that we practiced next to on a daily basis.

I started noticing trends in the students that I had that. They typically had the same sort of issues that I was having although my issues were much more exacerbated. I started noticing trends when people were showing up and when they lacked accountability it showed me that I was not showing up for myself either.

I also started to notice the subtle changes and shifting of energy within my own body and within my students. I knew what was best for them although I couldn't tell you how I knew it. I knew when things were going to happen and I didn't understand how I was able to know these things. My intuition started heightening. It was growing and growing and I didn't have anyone to talk about these things with. I didn't understand what it was or how it was happening and I kept it all to myself. Thinking it was just a part of life and if I ignored it then it would go away. Unfortunately my intuition, well not unfortunately, my intuition grew and grew and I just could not find anyone or anything to relate to. I started to confide in my husband about these things and it was about the same time that my teacher had told me that I should be doing Japa meditation on mala beads. This meditation increased my intuition dramatically, instantaneously. When I started to confide in my husband about these things he started displaying signs of rejection that started to weigh heavy on me. The more I confided in him the more he seemed to reject the idea of what I was doing, the path I was going in and me as a whole. At one point in time he had told me that he had felt I was in a cult and that I needed to stop doing yoga and meditation and get back to normal life.

This started a huge shift within me that started to pull two separate sides of me in different directions. I became very confused. I didn't know which way was right or wrong and had no idea what to do about any of it. Being married and being a mother and also being a Yogi practicing meditation and teaching others how to help themselves. I had to hold true to what I felt within my body and my mind, which was that I felt better about myself and what I was doing when I was practicing yoga and teaching. I started to separate from my marriage more and started to feel alienated when I was at home. The separation increased over time and our marriage seemed to start to fall apart slowly over the span of 4 years.

The more I focused on healing myself and my deep-seated wounds from my childhood, the more centered I felt. The more normal I felt. The more alive I felt! The more alive I felt the more I could feel, the more connected I felt to myself and to those around me. Before yoga I couldn't feel anything within my body, when I had given birth to my children I felt pain but couldn't tell you where the pain was exactly. I couldn't push when the doctors told me to push because I didn't know what that area of the body felt like. I had cut off all senses from my brain to the neck down. I was and felt completely numb within my physical body. I also was emotionally unavailable. I was there for my children and was almost overcompensating this emotional outpouring onto them and was unable to do it with any other human being or even with my own self. I had also been battling with my self worth as well. I had an internet business that was at one point the only way that we were able to pay our bills. Yet it always felt like it wasn't good enough for anyone especially for my husband and my family, especially my own mother. I had started this internet business as a way to pass time and to earn extra money when my husband was working and traveling and my kids were taking naps and then once they started school I wanted to fill my time even more as I'm someone that always needs to be productive and doing something. At the time that it was first created I had grossed six figures in nine months. It was something that astonished me and although it was a huge success I never got the recognition that I felt I deserved. My husband and my mother kept telling me that it wasn't a "real job." Without having health insurance it wasn't a real job. It always weighed heavily on me and at the point where we were at this moment I had the yoga studio and we're still doing and running this internet business out of the house. Nothing I did was good enough for anyone. I know now that it was a reflection of how I felt about myself that they were just showing back to me but nonetheless it still hurt tremendously to not have the people I cared about most backing me up or showing me any sort of support.

I had started to realize that my back pain, the deeper rooted pain that was showing itself to me was stemming from not feeling supported. I couldn't explain it but I just felt it. I knew I had to start creating my own foundation, one that was supported by myself instead of looking towards others for that support that I needed. I kept searching for outside sources of inspiration, for financial support and for emotional support and no one was giving it to me because I wasn't able to give it to myself. I didn't know how to do it for myself. But I had finally started to realize that I needed to try to search these things out for myself. The more I seem to look for my own answers from within the more friction and tension seem to show up within my marriage and with my relationships with my family. It felt like everyone was trying to keep me down and no one wanted me to be who I really was, me. Everyone wanted me to be who they wanted me to be, to follow the manual of how they wanted me to act. Any inclination of me finding my own way or being connected within my true self seemed to be a problem for them and their way of living life or how they thought life should be lived.

Yoga was something that was always there for me when I needed it the most. It didn't disappoint me, although it did show me things I really needed to work on that were really hard to look at most of the time, it was always there to support me no matter what. It didn't discriminate on what I looked like and although there were many times especially in the beginning that I used to compare myself to others, it was my own judgment of myself that kept me there. It was not something that someone else did to me but it was me taking accountability for myself and my own actions. Yoga was me. I *did* yoga. My relationships were getting harder and harder and I think it was because I was becoming closer connected with who I was really meant to be. That's what it felt like to me. No matter what anyone else was telling me, I knew deep down inside what yoga was doing for me and it was only for the better.

What makes Ashtanga yoga specifically beneficial was the fact that we did the same poses every day. It was the measurement to which I compared everything else in my day to. When I felt something in my physical body, I was able to start connecting it to my mind and the things I thought about. The negative thoughts about myself would manifest in different ways in my physical body. I was able to start to recognize these patterns of thoughts and of behaviors through my physical yoga practice. It was the most amazing thing to me to figure out these things within myself and then apply them to my students. That yoga mat was the single most life changing thing I have ever experienced, and I was in charge of it, it was me and no one else that could help me, that could process things and that could reveal the truth hidden underneath all of the layers of ignorance.

My constant, yoga
2020 Ocean City, NJ

15

Trying To Leave a Marriage

There were several times when I tried to leave my marriage. Some were small and some were big, leading up to the final one. These patterns were very hard for me to leave as they were so ingrained within me, within every ounce of me, within my DNA. Each time I left it got harder but it also got easier. The first time I left was years earlier and I barely remember what the circumstances were but it was me feeling like I was being neglected. I went and stayed with my mother for a couple of days before he begged me to come back to which I obliged. It was while living in Central New York that the other three break ups happened.

During July 2016 I was going through a phase of mourning. I had left Kage and had been staying at a friend's house for a couple of weeks. My friend's mother, who was like the only mother figure I ever had in my life, had passed away and I had only heard about the funeral a day too late. During the same time of the year we had visited Kage's grandfather in hospice and had seen both of my parents, although in different states. We had seen all of these people within a short week or two of each other. It was what felt like a very strange time. A lot of things felt like they were ending and there felt like a crumbling of foundations all around me.

I felt like I was losing my mind. I felt broken and lost and even though it was my decision to leave the marriage it was extremely hard for me to handle. I felt like I was pushed so far over the edge that I literally had no other choice but to leave for my own sanity. I was crying all night for periods of 3 to 4 days in a row. Anytime we tried to communicate with each other all we did was argue. I was having a hard time sleeping and when I went to the yoga studio I prayed that no students would show up and it worked. It was for the better for at least a week or two because I was in such a terrible spot. Then the lack of students started affecting me in a negative way. I didn't want them to show up because I felt so terrible but then in the same thought process I was upset that nobody was there and I felt even more alone. I felt like the universe was trying to tell me to let go of the studio and to let go of the students that I had become attached to.

I have been nervous to tell my parents about leaving my husband and I was shocked to hear their responses once I did have enough guts to speak with them. My mother said *can't you just stay together for the sake of the kids?* My father only asked if I had told the kids and was concerned about their reactions. Both were very odd responses since neither of them seem to have cared about those things when they got divorced and separated our family. And neither one of them validated my feelings or what I was going through. It was as a result of their own shortcomings that made them act the way they did towards me. They didn't want me to do what they did and they never once saw things from my point of view. That's all I wanted. I didn't get it and so there was always a feeling of not being understood by them, feeling lost and confused and totally utterly alone with only myself and my own pain and suffering keeping me company. My mother sent me $40 and then continued to act like nothing ever happened trying to ignore anything that she didn't want to deal with personally. Which was not much.

I then started mourning the loss of my parents though they were still amongst the living. Each has shown their lives moving forward without ever looking back at the children they created. I was located in the past for them and they had both left me there. I felt abandoned and I had only been 38 years old. I have never had a relationship with either of them worthy of any positive thoughts up until that point. I had always hoped that I would get that eventually but at last here they were moving on without me. I suppose it's ironic or a coincidence that within the span of two weeks I have had to let go of everything and everyone that I've ever known for the past 38 years of my life.

It was as if I was dying or at least that version of me was dying. I always envied Kages for having a picturesque family, though loosing both his parents who had passed away when he was younger I didn't envy. I have never understood why he was in so much pain. After all, I had thought that I went through pain and suffering much worse than him and thought he was lucky for not having been through what I had. I had a bed that he had two parents that loved and showed him love. They did everything they could for him. My parents seem to have done nothing and everything despite me. I had to learn that one man's pain is evenly as terrible as another's. No matter what it is. All of our pain has done things to us and made us who we were. All I wanted was another human beings unconditional love and mostly from my parents, especially from my parents. Whether they are living or past, it's something that if we don't feel like we have, then it feels like we are incomplete. Constantly searching for love outside of ourselves as a result of not being able to have it in the present moment from the people that created us and gave us life. I have spent 38 years seeking approval and love from others who are so easily unwilling to give it back to me. It's almost a bittersweet ending to a previous life.

We had spent a couple of months apart and I eventually ended up returning back home. We basically told the kids that I was just away doing yoga stuff and so they never knew the difference although I'm sure they felt it and just wasn't consciously aware of where the pain and suffering was coming from.

Valentines Day 2017

When we broke up this time I didn't tell anyone. I waited a few days until I told anyone because we broke up on Valentine's Day, it was the middle of the week, and really who cared about the crap I was going through. Especially since it's the fourth time we broke up. History repeats itself until you learn the lessons you are supposed to learn. I was finally willing to learn them this time, and so glad because it was about time. I surrendered and was now about to deal with the circumstances of the decision.

I told my sister, and my friend Dana. Neither found it to be that big of a deal considering it was just the same thing happening yet again. I told them this time will be different. It already was different because it actually wasn't even my idea. Of course I had already been thinking about it. For months. I was trying to figure out what to do. I had already changed my whole lifestyle, to do my best to avoid him. For 2 years I had woken up early to go practice and teach yoga, and I would come home and take a nap so I would be well rested enough to stay up for him and the kids at night. But as the time went on, and I had changed so many things for him, I started noticing that no matter what I did, it was never good enough for him. He always found fault with things, with everything, except himself. And so over the years and the last 3 break ups, would be the only time he would ever listen to when I spoke. He would change or listen to what I would say and it would be great for a while but then it went back to the "norm". I finally realized this time that I don't want to change for him, why should I change what he thinks is not good enough. And I didnt want him to change for me either. I have done so much changing for myself, for the better, and as it went on, he liked me less and less, and found more fault in me with every break through or healing moment I had had.

I was so miserable that I purposely went into yoga earlier and earlier. I woke up at 3:30 and would be on my mat practicing at 5am, usually after already doing my daily japa meditation. On Sunday and Mondays when he had off, I would make sure to go in a little later, and stay longer. I would then go and sit at the cafe downstairs for hours. I would eat, drink chai, read and write until the place got so crowded and overrun with college kids that it would end up being annoying to hang out at. Sometimes I would go back to the studio which was on the second floor right above the cafe and just spend more time there by myself or I would go and get the kids donuts and bring them home. Usually the kids would be awake already, and Kage would still be sleeping.

One day we decided to take his car to go out, which I had previously used to go to work in the morning for some reason. Usually it was because the van did not heat up and at 4am it's cold in north NY in the winter. This time he went to sit in the front seat and once he realized the seat was not pushed back to his liking, he flipped out on me. I asked why it was such a big deal, and he said, and I quote "If you change the seat, you need to change it back to exactly where it was for me." I not only did not understand why he was throwing a hissy fit and couldn't just easily change it back himself, but the bigger question was, how could I change it back to the way he likes it if I don't know where it was? It's not like it was a programmable setting that can be adjusted. The fact that I even replied to him was an issue because arguing was his middle name. And boy he was real good at it. We argued in circles, always, and this time was no different. It kept going and going. I always gave in, but I told myself I wasn't giving in to this argument, it's totally ridiculous! But you know what happened? He had beaten me down with his words, and I just couldn't take it anymore. We were in the car driving for half an hour already and I had to make a choice. Either tell him he's right and move on, and try to enjoy time with the kids, or let the argument last...forever. Because he never apologized. It just didn't happen because he always wanted to be right, about everything. I wish I could say this was the most ridiculous argument we had...I think it maybe actually. There is another one that frequently came up that's just as stupid, and it's me not throwing my tea bags out in the trash when he wanted me to.

I was the one who did the dishes, so why was it so offensive to him that I did it when he looked in the sink in the morning, or at night? He didn't deal with it. But it was his need for control that did deal with it.

We argued that one to death. And I would purposely throw them out, I ended up tiptoeing around the way I lived because I was scared of his reactions to things I did. I mean, even drinking tea made me resent him and there was nothing I could do about it. It didn't change, even with therapy together. I swear the therapist had a crush on him, in case I haven't mentioned it before. She would laugh at his jokes, and always had a smirk on her face when she talked to him. She wouldn't call him out on his stuff, and when things got to me and my behavior, she was always pressing my buttons.

These things happened more and more and our happy times happened less and less.

The time came where I would make sure I was in bed before he got home from work. It wasn't that hard really. I had asked him for at least 6 months to try to get home earlier to spend time with us since he would not get home till around 9pm during the week. Which I never understood considering they stopped taking clients at 6:30 pm. Regardless, my and our families' needs went unanswered. His response started out as " Let's wait til work slows down," and then it went to "I'll think about it in a few months," then it went to "You never asked me to change my schedule." which I hate to say happens often. He often accused me of saying things I never said, or saying things never happened that in fact did happen. It started happening so often that I legit thought I was going crazy. Until one day I decided to start documenting the stuff. Turns out, I wasn't crazy. I can't believe I stayed for so long. So many women are stuck in these marriages and can't leave because they did what they thought they were "supposed" to do. They are supposed to stay home, have the kids, raise the kids, and be the silent partner in all the husband's needs to fill his big head. Get a good job, make good money, buy a big house, a fancy SUV, have a big flat screen, and hang it on the wall. And let's not forget, they do "all" the work...we have it easy..right? Laugh out loud. What's easy about pushing out a 7.9 pound and a 9.10 pound baby with no epidural. Having your vagina split open almost the whole way back to your anus. What's easy about getting yelled at by the La Leche group in the hospital when they catch you feeding your baby formula (mind you which was after I already breastfed and wasn't producing enough milk because my body was in a constant state of fight or flight) What's easy about having no sleep except in 2 hour increments? What's easy about putting 3 people ahead of yourself and sacrificing your own goals and self care to take care of everyone else around you?

So things were bad. I was so over therapy, it started to go nowhere. I told him he should go without me as I had an appt or something. He went and said that the therapist said he was fine and there was no need for him to come on his own. I almost lost it. It's absurd. Even "normal" people can use therapy, you need to get stuff out. You can always talk about something. Who knows what she actually said as I only got his version of it. But my mind was made up, I just had to figure out what to do. I tried to think of a million different things. I made only enough money to get by with teaching yoga, and get by, I mean by paying the rent for the studio, and paying for a few coffees, a few meals and gas to and fro. It was nothing. I looked for jobs all the time and there was nothing above minimum wage. Nothing that allowed me to get on my feet.

My birthday is on February 9th and then the 14th is Valentine's Day. He usually combined the two. Like when we went to Atlantic City when we got engaged, or the year after when he took me to Disney. But over the years I had asked him not to get me any gifts for any holidays, which he usually ignored. And this was no different. I don't need "things" because of a holiday. What I always wanted was just love and attention. Which I never got. Clearly. This time was no different. The day before my birthday, he didn't want to wait to give me my present so when he got home around 5pm, I was pretending to be asleep, and he woke me up and asked me to come downstairs.

He gave me my gift. We had gotten into a huge fight because he didn't think that I liked my gift enough to make him feel good.

A few days later and it's the 14th. I go to the spa and see the lady who has become my spiritual advisor. This spiritual lady, who has been through similar things as me, marriage, divorce, kids, new relationship, I started going to in order to get waxed. All of a sudden we are talking about deep, personal things. She is into spiritual stuff and asks me about yoga, and tells me about these speakers who have Youtube videos. She says you need to read this book *The Power of Now* by Eckhart Tolle and my response is, that's the 2nd or 3rd time someone told me to read that book. Maybe I should. She informs me about this guy who has a channel on Youtube, and that seems more my speed for right now. I'm already reading a bunch of books, and have more books lined up after these ones. That night I lay in my bed. I set up the iPad and type in his name. I see there are tons of videos and can't decide which one to choose. So I scroll and decide to just tap on one without reading the captions and that will be the one I'm supposed to watch. So I started watching it, and it's long. The beginning is boring. And then it starts to get interesting and my ears perk up. He is saying everything I need to hear. all of it. Then he gets to a certain part. I lose it, I start bawling my eyes out and just know it's what I need to do. I had to hear it. The timing was right.

It was Valentine's Day and Kage didn't leave a card for me, no text, no phone calls and I just didn't care anymore. I watched this video and saw my destiny. I needed to figure out how to get out. But how? How does one start to leave a partnership that is half their lives, almost 2 decades wrapped up in each other in every single way?

Kage comes home late. Super late. Wakes me up to give me flowers, and that's it. He throws them on the bed next to me, while I give him the look of discontent. At this point I resent every ounce of him.

Says to me

"I took off today but I went to work anyway."

I don't know what that's supposed to mean, except that he's even more of a dick than I thought he was. He finally comes out and says it.

"I can't be in a relationship like this."

Me either.

"Are you calling it quits?" He says... think about how he words that for a second. "You" calling it quits? He totally turned it around on me.

Sounds good to me, however he wants to say it.

I just couldn't do it anymore. I was miserable. I lived for the last few months trying to suck it up. I told myself I would stay here, in this terrible, loveless marriage, just for my kids sake. But I realized it did nothing for anyone. Not for me, that was obvious. Not for the kids, because me being miserable affected them, and made them unhappy. Not for Kage because me staying there prevented him from any sort of happiness as well, even if I was the only person to see it.

I drank months, even a year or 2 away because I hated life. But now that I was sober, I couldn't distract myself with alcoholism.

For now what's best for the kids is for them to be in a stable place. Which unfortunately is there, without me. Thomas needs his support at school and we (Thomas and I) have worked really hard at creating a great place for him to thrive. He's in school more than he is with anyone else, so that is the most important thing right now. Same for my daughter as well. Although I really wish she didn't have to be there. I don't want either of them to be there but he wouldn't let me take them out of the state, and unfortunately I can't do anything about that.

I ended up staying at the house from February until April 1st. I was trying to stay longer but he told me I needed to leave and kicked me out. I wanted to leave, but I just had no idea where to go or what to do. There were no jobs coming to me, I couldn't even get an interview.

Since I could not find a place to work out where I could afford my own place I had no other choice but to move in with my sister in Philadelphia. The unfortunate part about this was that she lived 4 1/2 hours away from Central New York where my kids lived. At the time I really had no other choice but to leave and to try to start my life over again. It was something that I regretted for over a year as I really found it difficult to not judge myself and the pain that I had inflicted on my own children. I know that they did not understand what happened and that we hid things from them because we thought it would be better for them to not witness our arguing but I understand now that by not letting them witness anything at all that it caused even more of an issue within our lives. They were not able to see us argue and they also never saw resolution either. I had always been around a mother that screamed and yelled and never wanted to put my own children in that scenario. We both thought we were doing the best for them but as a result of that things were very confusing when I left. We were both very confused about the marriage ending and the last thing we understood how to do was communicate that to our children. We did go to counseling together and tried to ask for advice on how to speak to them about it and we followed those directions. But still as I look back today there are still unresolved things and I definitely got blamed for all of them. Because I was the one that left the physical family unit I got blamed for everything, even though I was the one that got kicked out.

The other hard thing to deal with was the repercussions from my friends and family. I had my two closest best friends tell me straight to my face that they thought I was doing a terrible thing and that I was an awful parent and mother for doing so. Neither one of them was living my life and neither one of them understood what I was going through. One of them I never spoke to again, I guess she just judged me so much that she could not get over it and be my friend anymore. My other friend I know voiced these things to me because she was in a similar situation and wanted to leave her marriage but we're staying just for the sake of the children. I don't blame either of them for reacting to me the way they did but it also did not help me feel supported in any way by anyone.

There is no harder decision that I've ever had in my entire life than that one. Mother leaving their children behind is not something that anyone can ever comprehend unless you have lived it and experienced it for yourself. I was always very hard on myself and this was no different.

The year after moving out was the hardest year of my life. I cried pretty much every single day, I told myself how much I hated myself, I wanted my life to be taken from me because I felt like I was the worst person that had ever lived. I felt like I had caused so much pain to everyone around me that I didn't deserve to live. I was in so much pain.

April 1st I had to leave New York. I had two garbage bags filled with clothes, a couple of plants, some artwork and books and that's all. That's all the belongings I had been able to fit in my car. I packed the car and left to move in with my sister at first. My mom made it clear that she did not want me there at her house and so my sister allowed me to be with her until I found a job to start paying her rent. Unfortunately, that only lasted about two weeks. Things there are a bit complicated and I'm gonna leave that out but what happened was we got into a fight and I had nowhere else to go and so I told my mom I was on my way. I didn't want to be there because I knew that it wasn't going to be a healthy place to be, especially given the fact of how I came to be there and the very unstable state in which I was living. Being around anything ungrounding is not beneficial for someone that was going through what I was dealing with. She had also made it clear that my children were not welcome there either. Something they felt when they came there for my visitation and eventually refused to come visit.

Before leaving Central New York I told my yoga students that I was going to be leaving and one student I had been teaching how to assist the students so that she could take over the studio all together. We had spent the good part of February and March going over these things so the transition would hopefully become smooth for all of them. It did last at least a month after I had left but the person that took it over eventually texted me and said that she was very angry with me that I moved and did not contact her to see how she was doing and told me that she wanted nothing else to do at the studio and that she was closing it down for good. I was in complete shock because she was mad at me for not reaching out to her when I was the one that felt that people should have been asking me how I was doing. No one asked how I was doing, no one cared about how I was or what I was going through. I was being blamed for all the pain in my family and no one wanted to stop to think about what had caused me to make this type of dramatic decision in my life. I was in shock that she was blaming me for something while I was going through something that I had no way to work through. I had no support system outside of my mother providing a house and a roof to live under. I had no one and nothing. But I guess once again she was reflecting back to me what I needed to see. I had started to see a resemblance between my leaving my husband and a friend who had left her partner many years earlier. The same exact thing happened and although I did try to reach out to her after she had left her family behind I quickly gave up because I had no idea how to be there for her. I never blamed her although she still thinks to this day that I blamed her but I didn't. I just didn't know how to be there for someone that was going through that kind of situation. I had never experienced it and had no idea how to be there for someone. I was starting to see that I needed to experience this because not only did I need to be a support system for myself but I also needed to experience it so that others had someone to talk to who went through the same thing. I would be ready for them when they were ready to leave their husbands. Only I didn't see that while I was going through it. I felt like I was completely alone. I had to experience this alone and I hated every single moment of it.

As I sat there in my moms house I would cry and break down looking at her bookshelves and seeing all of the self-help books, the Alcoholics Anonymous books. All of these things were a reminder that I was my mothers daughter. I felt so empty and I could not stop crying.

One day I lay in bed staring up at the ceiling. It's about 90 degrees and I am lying there unable to put the air conditioning on because my mother doesn't want to pay for it. Even after I told her that I would pay for it she still wouldn't let me. I lay their butt naked on the bed breathing heavy with drops of sweat pouring down my body onto the mattress. As I lay there staring out the window I wondered how many liquor stores there were nearby and which ones were open. All I wanted to do was drink away my pain to numb myself. All of a sudden it started to downpour. Rain was a deterrent for me to go outside. I lay there, my head going around and around in circles and I tried to think about taking it a step further. I thought about ending my life and the ways in which I could make that happen. The problems were that I wanted it to happen but in a way that I could guarantee death and that I wouldn't live through a suicide attempt and have to walk through life with some sort of abnormality. I didn't want to risk walking with only one leg or not having use of my appendages. I wanted an absolute guarantee that I would be able to transition into the other side and end this terrible, painful life full of suffering. I thought of all of the ways of all the pills I could get my hands on of the different ways I could try to strangle myself. As I went through all of these things within my mind I was too scared of the uncertainty that I wouldn't be able to complete it and be guaranteed a state of death. As I lay there I tried to think of the people that I could reach out to for help. I really came up with no one except for a man that I had recently met and so I finally after going back and forth to give him a call. He helped me get through that evening and it did not result in me going to the liquor store or an attempt at taking my life. Thankfully, after that event it was pretty much on the uphill. I mean how much further down can you go? The only further down you could go is literally by taking your own life. I am thankful that I didn't have to take it that far although I know I wasn't so lucky in many of my previous lives that I have lived.

After my hormones started to even out I realized what the main problem was. It wasn't only the depression and the experiences I was going through but it was also an imbalance that had been caused by my birth control pill that I recently had gone on. I started googling it and sure enough it is plain as day as a side effect of birth control. I couldn't believe that a side effect of birth control was wanting to take your own life. There it was right in the pamphlet of the birth control itself. Why was no one talking about this, why was no one disgusted, the fact that this can have such a dramatic effect on our brains and how we think.

Why was this not more well-known? Well here it is I'm saying it now, I immediately went off the pill and had never felt as unstable as I did in that moment. I do know for a fact that my mental state and the unbalancedness was only exaggerated by the hormones of the pill. I would never recommend that for anyone, ever. It took some time for the pills to move through and out of my system but I felt like a whole completely different person after that cleansing.

I decided that I just need to focus, show up for my yoga practice every day and be the best I could be at the yoga studio, my new yoga studio, my new job, and my new schooling that was about to start soon.

16

Consequences of Divorce

I had an appointment with a divorce attorney from New York. Needless to say it didn't go exactly as I had wanted it to go. I went into it all gung ho- like everything I ever wanted was going to come true and everything would go my way. She would ask me what I wanted and tell me that it's no problem. After all, it seems like it's a great time to be a woman in this world. With everyone talking about feminism, even the men. Everyone is for women's rights these days, it's about time.

Boy was I dead wrong.

Her: Why did you leave the house?

Me: Because it was not a marriage I could be in any longer.

Her: But he wasn't abusive?

Me: He was manipulative.

Her: Why did you leave the state?

Me: I had nowhere else to go, he wanted me to leave the house and it was not an environment that was good any longer. I moved in with my parents because I had nowhere to go, no money, and no job.

Her: Well you will never get the kids now. My suggestion is if you want the kids, you need to move back into the house and get a job. Save up to get on your feet and then take the kids. That's the only way.

Me: He wouldn't let me back in the house. And he made me sleep on the floor.

Her: He can't make you do anything. You own the house too, he can't keep you out.

Me: But we hate each other and can't be around each other.

Her: He can come after you for child support and you will have to pay it even without a job.

Me: But I just spent 12 years supporting him while he went after his dreams and desires of working and I ignored mine to be a stay at home mother? How can this happen to me after I gave up my whole life for him and for them?

Her: My advice then is to do nothing. Let him make the first move. If he serves you papers then call me right away and we will get on top of it asap.

It didn't make any sense to me. I had another attorney after that and she did the same exact thing to me, only worse. I was shocked at how evil and vindictive they wanted me to be towards my ex. He was the father of my children, I didn't want to try to win, for winning sake, and I certainly wasn't trying to get anything from him except what I needed to start over. I also didn't want jeopardize our relationship for the future. I was tied to him for the rest of our lives and the last thing I am going to do to someone who likes fighting, is fight. I didn't want to fight. I didn't think it was right and I certainly didn't have the money to pay for it or the energy to do it. It wasn't about ego for me. he could have everything for all I cared, I just needed something to start over. Everything I ever owned except what I could fit into my car was in that state. I cared only for my children and to be able to buy food for myself until I could get back onto my feet, myself. After all the attorneys, him and I decided to work it out ourselves and pay one attorney to do all the paperwork, one of his clients. We went back and forth and were able to come up with something. Something I still don't regret, even though people told me I was crazy. I felt it in my heart that fighting for more was not in the best interest of the future for our relationship, and our children. I let go of any attachment for more and of my own ego. Something, that today I am happy to say has come completely full circle as we are able to communicate and get along extremely well, after years of toxic communication and blaming on both our parts. Had I tried to fight, it never would have ended. There is a time and place for fighting, and that was not it.

17

Feeling The Numb

It's December, and it's only a slightly cold morning in Fishtown at 6 in the morning. I only recently learned about what EDS is and I have to come back to my yoga mat differently. Not like I have before, at least 1800 times before, today is different. I am still the same I was yesterday and the day before and the day before that. Or am I?

I roledl out my mat and as I stand there, I can already feel the trouble in my feet before I even begin. I inhale, bring my hands up towards the sky and I have to resist the urge, where the easiness lies, to let my shoulder blades come up towards my ears. I exhale, fold forward and I have to resist the urge, where the easiness lies, to touch my flat hands to the ground and touch my face to my knees.

Inhale, head up and resist the urge again. Exhale, jump back, as my bones crack. Inhale, upward facing dog, as my left elbow cracks. Exhale, downward facing dog as both my legs crack.

My right thumb cracks constantly during my practice. My left shoulder blade needs to be readjusted constantly. My cervical spine bows left, my thoracic bows right. My right shoulder folds inward. My left pelvis tilts up and back.

Now that I have spent years trying to go inward, I have finally arrived here. I ask myself, *Have I always cracked like this or am I just now paying attention to the noises? Is it my age, has it gotten worse and worse over time? What am I doing, am I doing it right or am I only hurting myself worse.* I reach a standing pose quickly after recently deciding that I need to cut out most of them due to the SI joint instability. Only doing poses where my hips are stabilized. I attempt to stand on one leg, starting with the worse one first. The left. I lift my right leg up to grab my right toe and then it happens. My left ankle cracks and then I can instantly feel the tingling and numbness go around my foot and up my calf only slightly. Oh, so that's how it happens.

I finally begin to feel numb. I can feel my greatest body achievement, that I had taken no part in achieving, turning out to be my greatest weakness. My flexibility. I'm elastic. I'm weak. My tissues are soft, moldable, pliable, loose, lax, weak. They are all weak. They allow outside influences to do anything to them that they wish. Two and a half years of symptoms and I can finally pinpoint it. Something. Anything. 6 years of practice with lots of pain. Lots of pain, here, there, back here again. In the body, in the mind. And what does it all mean? I've been at a point now that it's been years and it never goes away. I have tried to work harder and harder to try to make it stop or at least feel better, or improve. There was one week last year. And I just had another week. I want it longer.

I want to accept it. I have accepted it. I don't complain about it. I'm sick of it. I'm ok. I'm not ok.

Is it my karma, is it fate, is it the universe telling me something. I don't know. I just want to give up. I'm sick of it. You're not going to beat me, I will destroy you. I will prove that chronic diseases can be cured. Just watch me.

I wake up and the tingling cold numb is gone. Every morning is like the movie Groundhog Day. Starting all over, and repeating, yet differently. I'm usually ok until I get to the mat, or sometimes not until hours after. It's walking and I know it. But just not walking is not an option. By midday my feet feel like they are frozen. I crank the heat in the car as I drive home from work to try to bring feeling back to them, but it never works. It just calms my mind until I start to sweat from the mid part of my back so I turn it off. Feeling the numb comes and goes like an unfriendly ghost. It wasn't invited but it wants to make its presence known.

I go to the chiropractor often for adjustments and hear just ow crooked my physical body is. I am making it my life mission to straighten myself out, through my body and then also the mind and spirit. No one knows what to do with me, they try and try to offer solutions, some work a little bit, some not at all. Try everything I can to become stronger, instead of being hyper mobile and stretched beyond my limits to become in so much pain, discomfort and numbness. I just feel it within me. I can feel that I have the answers, I just don't know how to reach in and grab them. I will not give up though. My determination, drive and self discipline has only shown me that I am capable of any-thing as long as I just keep going.

18

Emergency Room Visit

Well what can I say as I sit here, in bed, 8 o'clock on a Monday night, in a bed, in a room in my mothers house. It's been awhile since I wrote anything, anything at all. Apparently it's overdue as I spent virtually the entire day in the emergency room alone.

I've been having symptoms for months. But it really started about 6 weeks ago. I had a dramatic drop in my energy levels. I was exhausted and extremely fatigued. I went from practicing yoga for a good hour and half, and feeling excellent, to all of a sudden, I can barely do 30 minutes. And that 30 minutes was very difficult. I mean very. Fatigue sucks. I feel like I have no control over it. I hate not having control over things that I cannot see. I am on Day 4 of blurry vision and my right eye feels better though things like books, or even reading what I am typing here is too blurry to read. I can, however, keep typing it. It just looks like a bunch of text overlapping. My eyes were crusty this morning, a symptom that seems to have come out of nowhere. My eyes feel like they are bulging out of my head, I can feel the pressure behind my eyes.

Being in the Emergency room sure has brought up some tough things to think about. You know I have barely gotten sick since I started practicing Ashtanga yoga and then I ended up in the ER. The tests they ran at the hospital all came back normal but I know it was a thyroid and hormone issue caused by losing so much energy by energy vampires. Specifically the person I was dating, mixed in with the birth control pills, I tried a smaller dose and went back on them. It just didn't work for me. my body was screaming at me. Screaming to change things in my life, to turn it around. I was giving too much of my energy away to this man. Trying so hard and putting energy into someone that wasn't reciprocating it. Why was I doing this? The nurse said there was nothing wrong with me, that it was stress related and they discharged me after spending the entire day there while they ran all the tests. Let me tell you something, you cannot compare my normal range to everyone else's range. Clearly there was an imbalance or my eyes wouldn't be bulging out of my skull. The person I dated didn't even come to see me at the hospital, who was in school to become a nurse. Yup. I picked him, of all people. I knew I was right, there was something wrong, and ruled out my eyes were the problem after going to the eye doctor before the ER. I left the hospital, took blood sugar levels, wondering if it was diabetes that runs in my family, on my fathers side and that didn't help either. I decided to buy vitamins that I found may help on the internet and sure enough, I took them and within the next day I felt a million times better. My body was not taking in energy, it was giving it all away to everyone and everything else. I was causing everything to be haywire and I had to fix it and get myself back on track, and strengthen myself and my boundaries, and clearly, my nutrition. I broke up with the guy I was dating and felt even better. I deserve better. I deserve to take care and focus on myself, instead of someone else. I needed to learn how, more, and so I did.

I had so many layers of hiding, from everyone else, and even myself. Layers and layers of hiding.

Who am I..really? To myself and according to others.

What do I have left? Thoughts. Lots of thoughts.

Attention seeking/Sex addict. Addicted to Yoga. Addicted to Eating. Addicted to Buying things/ collecting. Addicted to Drugs/ alcohol. Addicted to healing even. Addicted to trying to be perfect. I have had to overcome all of these things, one at a time.

At this moment, as I write, I believe that all illness is caused by an imbalance. This is obvious to most. But what is not obvious to many is that it starts with the internal thought energies first and then it leaks out into the physical forms. I can only speak of that which I have personally experienced, and like me, you may not be able to understand where I am coming from if you have not been fortunate enough to be as sensitive as I. But maybe something in here will resonate, even if it's just a little.

In Ashtanga yoga we often talk about how we are peeling the layers of an onion and I have always felt like that. Metaphorically and physically. From that first yoga class when I literally wore 2 layers of everything in order to feel safe by hiding my physical body. I didn't want to have anyone look at me, or anyone see me as a female that could be harmed. I didn't want to be hurt and so I thought if I hid my breasts, my legs and my skin then no one would see me and I would be safe. Now in yoga class, years later, I sometimes wear less clothes then I do to the beach. Just physical proof as to how far I have come in the process of peeling the layers of onion that is the self.

Recently, I have been having problems with my relationships. Any relationship. Every relationship. I am oddly compassionate to people I don't know and yet somewhat uncompassionate to those I know well. Besides my children. Although that can certainly be argued either way too.

I have always been really good at being alone. I have always been alone. Growing up, we were left alone. Once I went to college, I was alone. I did everything myself. I had to. I met my ex husband at college who toured around the world for 15 years while I raised our kids. I was good at being alone. I liked being alone. I wanted to just be left alone. It's no coincidence that once he stopped his profession and started a new one that required him being home, did our relationship really start to suffer. I was never happy with the way things "are" or "were". Always complaining about what I didn't have, until I had it and then found something else to complain about.

I was constantly looking for something to complain about and didn't even realize just how much I was only hurting myself by doing so. So I look at myself now. Now that I have changed so much from all of that, and what is happening is the same pattern. What relationships do

I have and how am I cultivating them? All my bestest friends are ones that live nowhere near me. I started to find myself being jealous of the friendships others have. People who talk to their friends everyday. People who ask others if they want to hang out. Those people don't ask me.

I have isolated myself so deeply that I became ok with it. Then I convinced myself it was the only way I could be happy. Convincing myself that the only way I could be happy is by making myself happy. Finding that when I have tried to be happy with another person, I went the complete opposite way and gave all of myself to a lover and ended up being very sick or hospitalized every time for it. I would rather be isolated and feel safe than giving myself away and having to go back to the ER.

I haven't been able to find a perfect balance to a thing that I am highly sensitive to. So now is the time. I think it's the missing link between who I want to be and who I am right now. Having gone through so many layers and leaving one very important layer left. The one very last thing that makes everything else that came before it the reason for my hiding. For creating the layers. Relationships.

In order to move forwards, I need to go backwards so that is what my journalled autobiography has been all about. It has helped me to see the way the things that happened to me affected me, and how by recognizing them I have been able to start healing from them. So why am I stuck where I am now?

I want a deeper connection to others. I am ready and willing to try.

19

Trying to date

One thing that kept coming to me from the people I did try to connect with, old friends and making new friends, was that perhaps it was time to start dating again even if it was only to try to forget about being away from my children. It was coming at me from almost every angle. I couldn't even think about dating like what it would look like. What would that feel like? I just couldn't even imagine it. I just wanted to be alone and I was starting to like the suffering in my aloneness. But that can only go on for so long because I had to be the one to pull myself out of it. And so I asked how is one day in this day and age? A good friend had suggested dating apps. And so that's where I started. I guess I got lucky, because the first person I met I ended up being in a relationship with though he lived an hour away from me. We still would see each other once a week and it went on for about three months. Learning about patterns of behavior through my own healing and through what I had experienced with my marriage I decided that I had a limit to how many I would ignore something or at least give them an opportunity to change or grow from the experience or from the pattern of behavior that was unhealthy. This was no exception and so I told myself that I would limit it to three. That if I gave someone the opportunity to grow and change by the third time if nothing had progressed then it was time for me to walk away and to move on.

The first relationship showed me all of the things that were still unhealed within me. It also made me prove to myself whether or not I was willing to stand up for what I wanted and what I felt I was worth to another person in a relationship. I had to end it as things were not the way they appeared at first and overtime they slowly started to reveal themselves to me. After that relationship I did not want to go back on dating apps nor did I want to try to date again either. A few months later, I found myself meeting someone through the natural way of interactions. That also went through the same motions as it showed me other things that were not healed although it did show me that I was attracting more of a balanced type of person. But just as before about three months went by and things started to unravel rather quickly. The things that I was trying to ignore were making themselves known and started to become very loud. Again, I had to take action and all those were extremely emotional for me and very hard in that moment, I had to leave that relationship as well. I knew I deserved more and it wasn't being shown to me through my relationships and so I went back to myself again to do more inner work. With each relationship and interaction I would see the reflection they were showing me, that I didn't like, that would get loud, to the point I had to see it in myself and go back to the drawing board. More inner work, more focus, deeper and deeper I went into my past, my trauma, my mind and into deep rooted things that were showing up that I seemed to be storing in my subconscious. These things wanted to be healed, or they wouldn't have sparked such a trigger within me. I had to keep taking action, not blame them, only look at the messages and move on and left my emotions on the mat after they made their way through my body and my energy field, sometimes as crying, sometimes as just air I exhaled.

A few months after that I decided to go back on dating apps, went on a few dates and had been seeing a couple people often but nothing serious and nothing even remotely emotional at all. One of the men was very well-off, worked for himself and was a true gentleman in every fashion of the word. He was extremely noncommittal as was I but I started to have feelings for him that he was not ready to reciprocate in that kind of way. I went back-and-forth trying to decide if I wanted to keep giving myself away sexually to someone that I knew wouldn't ever be at the same level or commit. Although he had all of the things, good looks and financial abundance it just wasn't something that I was willing to settle for. He was happy with taking care of me financially if I would be there and show up they way he wanted me to. I wanted something more. He didn't want to give that to me and so I ended that as well.

My divorce was eventually finalized and as required Kage put all the belongings he could find of mine into the garage so that I could drive up there and load up a U-Haul and bring it back down to Philadelphia. I had nowhere to store any of the stuff and so I ended up putting it into my grandmother's basement until I could move out on my own and had space to fill.

It felt like a great release getting some of those things back. A lot of the things that were left for me I had to call a dump truck to come pick it up and trash it because there wasn't enough room in the U-Haul for everything. I had to stick to what was most important. As I look back upon it now it's probably the best thing that could've happened. Although it was sad to have to leave so many things for the trash even after I had already left things for the trash the first time I left, it was as if I was releasing bits and pieces of my past and letting them be transmitted into the future or into becoming something else, something more useful for someone else. Or being buried into the dirt never to be seen again. It wasn't the first time and it definitely wasn't the last time.

Having the divorce finished felt very empowering to me. It helped me have more energy and put a step into my efforts of moving forward into my new future. Not having anything left there as far as belongings go, made me feel like I was living more in the present moment and not so much in the past.

20

Letting Go

It was through yoga that I started to realize just how much my mind was affecting my physical body. I have spent years and years doing the same things over and over again through my yoga practice and didn't seem to get any better at a certain point. I seem to have gotten to a plateau and then started getting an enormous amount of pain through-out my body. Now that I had been in massage school and was study-ing the body and anatomy and physiology I started to realize things that weren't connected inside of myself. I had started to realize that parts of my body were in constant tension. There were muscles that were tense no matter what I did to stretch them or to make them more relaxed. I was completely unaware of just how disconnected my entire physical body was from my mind. As a result of trauma I had cut off pretty much all of my female body parts. There were also other parts of my body that were hyper mobile. There would be times when my yoga teacher would touch a muscle to tell me to contract it to start building up the muscle and it wouldn't contract no matter how hard I tried to make it work, the muscle would just not react in any way whatsoever like a muscle should. I had started to realize and put pieces of a puzzle together based on what was happening within my family genes and past experiences I have had throughout my life.

My mom had always told me about something called EDS or Ehlers Danlos syndrome. She had the hypermobility aspect of that syndrome and was diagnosed with it as well as other people in my family. I had never thought of being diagnosed for it or even thought at all about it affecting me in any way.

It was because of massage school, my own healing and yoga that I realized just how important everything is in relation to each other. Meaning the way our parents treat us, the way we grow up and live life, things that we experience, the thought patterns that we learn, the things that we say to ourselves in our own heads and also the behaviors that we exhibit. How the way we hold in our emotions and also how much stress we go through really affects our entire existence. How everything is a part of our whole. How something that my grandparents have gone through that may have been traumatic for them and have not worked through is still living within my DNA. It gets triggered in me every time something remotely similar happens within my own life. It has been scientifically proven as such. How did I not know this? How can we change this and stop this from affecting my own children?

There were things I could tell and understand were happening within me that I could not thoroughly explain. I just kept plugging away searching for answers feeling that things were getting closer and closer to me figuring it out. I had to unlearn everything that I had learned and I had to search for my own truths, through science, experience and only by learning to trust myself and my intuition. I couldn't take anyone else's word for anything anymore.

21

REIKI

I was extremely thankful for the yoga teacher I had in Philadelphia. She was someone that understood energy more than anyone else I had met. She also understood the female body more than anyone else I had previously studied with as well. In addition to all those things as if it couldn't get any better she also understood trauma in a way that most people did not. She has taught me many things and in all of these areas. I couldn't have been more thankful if I tried. It's been years and years since I have seen her and I think about her almost every day. I know that there's something still left there for me to figure out or to heal and I'm just not sure if I'm ready yet. I felt like I let her down and I also feel like she left herself down as well. I felt like I unraveled my psychic abilities and she rejected me. I felt that her mind was just not ready to go in those places. In fact, now I'm writing these words down. I'm shedding tears just thinking about her. She's one of the most amazing people I've ever met in my life. She was there for me when no one else was. She didn't judge me and showed me love that no one else could. I barely even knew her and she allowed me into her studio, allowed me to study with her and to learn everything from her without ever expecting anything in return. She was a rock for me and a foundation that helped me push through all of my addiction to suffering. I never would have made it through that part of my life without her.

I was with her for a couple of years and we had both changed and grown a lot but there came a time that I pushed past my suffering and realized that I needed to move on from her being my teacher and from the student base that was gravitating towards us both. I didn't feel like I resonated with any of them anymore and I needed to let go and move on. By this point I knew the time to go was when it hurt too much to stay. When there's nothing left except hurt and pain, then you have to cut the cord. When there is nothing benefiting either party, there's nothing left to do but walk away.

It was something that was very difficult but I know that she understood at least I hope she did. I don't know if she will ever understand how much she meant to me back then and even still to this day. I mean I'm having trouble just writing this without bawling my eyes out. That is proof to me that I have not yet fully moved on from that relationship. She was like a mother to me and like a best friend although we had a very businesslike type of relationship. I felt like I could confide in her when needed and I hope that she felt that for me as well.

It was having her as a teacher that allowed me to have space to work through things on my own, in my own way and in an unconventional way as well. During this time I was in massage school and started learning more and more about energy and energy healing. The more I was working on myself the more other things would come to the surface more quickly asking to be resolved. I became very good at identifying issues that came up and then would realize the most perfect way to resolve and heal them. It was time I had to become my own teacher. I couldn't look towards others for help anymore, I had to find the answers from within, again.

In massage school I had to take a class called Reiki. It was a part of our schooling and was required. Before walking into the class I remember saying to myself how I don't believe in this, it's a bunch of fake nonsense. But I gotta do it for school and on into the class I went to. I knew I was a highly sensitive person, I could feel everyone's stuff that was around me but I never understood it at all. It was in Reiki class that I had started to realize well sort of what was happening. The teacher didn't explain how to do it; she just wanted us to go ahead and do what we felt compelled to do. Something I am very thankful for because if someone tells you what to do it could often block your own intuitive ideas. As we got partnered up and took turns back-and-forth I would go to the certain areas of the body that I was drawn to and I would say the things I heard in my mind and also would explain the things I was seeing within the visions in my head. I was astonished time after time as to how these things correlated with what was actually going on within my partners. People started looking at me and wondering how on earth I was getting this information and I didn't know how to answer them.

I would put my hands near their head, close my eyes and wait. I would just be open to receive anything that came to me. I put my hands on one persons head and immediately saw an X-ray of his chins within my minds eye. I went down to his shins and just put my hands there, one leg at a time. When I was done I asked him what he felt and thought and he immediately started to have tears in his eyes. It was the first class I had had with him, so I didn't know anything about him at all. He sat up, lifted up his sweatpants and showed me his legs. He explained to me that months earlier, he had jumped out of a window to try to kill himself and broke both of his legs. He lived and decided to change his life around. *How did you know,* everyone asked me. Even I wanted to know as it happened over and over again with each person. I knew that one person had stomach issues. I felt things they felt, I saw parts of their body in my mind or I would get words in my head as to where I should place my hands to help direct energy within them.

I looked at the teacher for guidance and she had nothing to offer me. I was shocked as I had thought that she would be the one to help me understand what was happening to me but there I was, yet again, even more confused than when I had walked in on the first day. I had to believe in this. I couldn't doubt anymore that I was getting information from people and that it was extremely beneficial for them. I just didn't understand the concept of what I was doing or how to do it. I signed up for Reiki 2 the next month and it was just the same, even more intuition coming through and nothing yet to help me understand what was happening. The same teacher, yet again, had nothing to offer me.

I had gotten to the point where I could start to read people's minds and knew what they were going to say before they said it out loud. I didn't tell people this because it really scared me and I didn't want to scare other people as well. I later realized that I needed to set boundaries and so that is what I said out to do and when I created these boundaries I no longer felt other people's stuff when I went into public. I didn't have to hear other people's thoughts. I didn't have to feel other people's emotions and I didn't have to feel other people's ailments and illnesses. It took me quite some time to establish those boundaries but once established they cannot be taken down. As long as I keep giving to myself and reinforce my boundaries, they will always remain there.

Reiki was my first real introduction and just a snippet into my future of working with energy. I found it very limiting though. We were taught to connect tot he energy and help move the clients own energy through their body, but everyone would feel great for an hour or two and always go right back to the same they were before. I didn't see it do anything really beneficial for the long term. Thats not to say that it doesn't have long lasting affects, I just didn't experience that. I knew there was something more. I just had to find it and prove it to myself.

3

Creating New Patterns

22

Hypnotherapy

I was graduating from massage school and had also met someone that I was in a relationship with that I cared about very much. In this relationship I had realized even more things to work on within myself, but also realized that he had the same things to work through as well. He was someone that chose to work on these things with me and through our relationship. We were working on things both on an individual level and on a relationship level with each other, which was different then anyone else I had dated. Everyone else just projected things onto me and blamed me or would flat out deny any wrongdoing at all. This was a nice change. There were a lot of things that were starting to come together all at once. I had finished massage school, passed the state boards to get my license, found a job at a spa and found a house to move away from my mothers house. Things were starting to come together and I was creating a new foundation and a new life.

I was connecting more with myself, healing myself even deeper and then trying to share that with someone I was in a relationship with that was open to receiving.

As we went through our relationship and were working towards growing closer, the more information I would be getting intuitively about what he was doing and thinking about at all times. We were connecting in ways that crossed boundaries. But I guess when you're entangled with someone through a relationship you are open at all times. Or at least more open as opposed to someone that you're walking by on the street. I was also starting my yoga practice all over again, starting from the very beginning. Trying to trigger the right muscles to contract and the right muscles to release tension. It was very painstaking and extremely ego breaking to say the least. It was all for the better though as I had to retrain my body and my mind. I was also going to the chiropractor on a regular basis. As my boyfriend and I grew closer I started to have major trust issues. Not just because of the information I was getting through intuition but also based on my past trauma as well. Nothing I was doing seemed to get me past or through these things all the way. Just little layers at a time. Hypnotherapy kept coming into my periphery and so I decided to look into it a little further. As a constant student and dedicated seeker of knowledge and information I signed up for a program at Southwest Institute of Healing Arts for a diploma in "Integrative Healing Arts Practitioner" and focusing on Hypnotherapy. Since I was signed up for the program, I figured I should probably try to experience what it was before starting classes. I was in such full trust and had so much faith in the universe now that I got loans and grants for schooling for something I had never even experienced for myself. That is what blind faith is, and it always comes back around for the better. It had proven itself to me, so I trusted it.

I had found a Hypnotherapist on the Internet that was relatively close to where I lived and so I booked a session with him through his website. I chose him and his practice because he offered a free 1 hour session. I had no idea what hypnotherapy involved and so I couldn't imagine spending a couple hundred dollars an hour on something I didn't understand. I went to the session and he completely blew me away. I left there with such a profound change I couldn't describe it with words if I tried. Of course for the sake of this book, I will attempt it.

I had booked that session specifically to resolve the issue around trust. I wanted to understand and heal my issues about not trusting people but more importantly trusting men at all. What ended up coming up was that I had the most issues with trusting myself! It all started with the self first. The relationship was just a reflection. The hypnotherapist would ask me questions and it would literally take me seconds if not a minute to answer him. He could tell that I was arguing with myself within my own mind determining what words I should actually let out of my lips. He would ask me a question and I would get an answer in my mind and then immediately argue that answer to determine what would be the best possible answer that he wanted to hear and then eventually mumble some sort of words out. Nothing at all that had to do with the actual answer that I would get to begin with. He is an absolute genius because I had no idea that this was what I was doing until he helped me work through it. He would ask me a question and say, *Why are you taking so long?* I didn't know why. I wasn't even really aware that I was taking so long either. I was totally unaware. We ended up literally breaking down my entire thought process. I had no idea that my life had revolved around changing what I believed or had gotten intuitively for something that worked better for everyone else. Ignoring my own thoughts and changing who I was to satisfy someone else.

I revolved my answers and my life to fit the person that was around me, at all times. When I had gone through so much trauma it would make perfect sense as to why I ended up being that way. If I brought any attention to myself then I would be harmed or at least there would be the possibility of it. I needed everything to be easy for everyone else so that I could feel safe. I would alter things in an effort to keep confrontation at a minimum, at all times.

He started to help me break down all of these barriers. We went step-by-step in bringing back the pieces of myself that had been disassociated in order to try to find trust within myself again. I believe I was there for about two hours and what he did for me that day was not only establish trust within myself but also I created a direct link between my subconscious mind and my physical body. He helped me create a physiological response to a *yes* answer by moving one of my fingers. Meaning, anytime someone would ask me a question if I didn't know if it was a *yes* or a *no* my body would automatically tell me if it was a yes. It was an amazing trick and I tested it out frequently after leaving his office. Up until that point it was extremely difficult for me to make any decision regardless of how easy it was. Do I buy this color towel or that color towel? I could be staring at towels for an hour and it would not make it any easier for me to make a decision. I literally couldn't trust any decision I made. I was so afraid and in fear of making the wrong choice. The trauma I had created this behavior within me for survival and it dictated how I walked through life. I couldn't have picked out a set of towels in less than an hour if I had tried.

Having this little trick created a direct link to my subconscious mind and made me be able to tell what decision was best for me, without having to think about it. Without wasting time and energy.

I believe that this is one of those pivotal moments of my life. It made me fully connected to my intuition in a way that I had not experienced before. I couldn't tell previously if I was having an intuitive thought or if it was something that was created within my thinking brain. This was a way that bypassed my thinking brain. The thing that was interesting about the experience with my hypnotherapist was that at the time he didn't believe in past lives or anything outside of the current lifetime that we lived and I believed the same. We went just as far back as you could go, which was when I was born. The events that had been stuck within my mind that wanted to be released were very interesting and a few of them I had no conscious recollection of. It was really interesting to see that when you were in such a meditative state the types of things that can come to the surface. These things want to be healed and want to be let go of. We first started at the age of 12 and then went back to the age of 5 then 2 and then the age of 1 before going to my birth. It seems like we had reached a limit and that's all that we could've done pertaining to this specific event with resolving trust. He then created an audio for me to listen to as I fall asleep every night for 21 days to change the thought patterns pertaining to trust that I went home with. He told me to shoot him a message when I had completed the 21 days. Well it was on the 21st day, on the last day, as I fell asleep listening to the audio my body started convulsing. I couldn't explain exactly what had happened but I knew it had something with the nervous system as that was pretty obvious because of having the experience and knowledge of massage school and yoga. It had created a dramatic effect within my mind and my body and I became fascinated with the idea of this modality and I was excited that I trusted my reflection and intuition and had signed up to go back to school once again to study hypnotherapy.

Before the online school started I found a workshop in Utah that I was very excited to attend as well. I didn't know anything about the person putting it on but it sounded like it was an opportunity for me to learn a lot from about resaving trauma.

The issue with trust within myself started to get better and better, I still had a lot of work to do however, especially in trusting people around me. I trusted strangers more then I trusted my boyfriend or the ones closer to me. Something that came back to haunt me later on in life (insert foreshadowing for book 2). My boyfriend and I still had issues, though we continued to work on them. Hypnotherapy helped me to trust myself and the more intuitive hits I got pertaining to my relationship, the more I became confrontational about them instead of ignoring them or thinking that I was making it up out of my low self esteem. I would start to see and fell more, and became more and more sensitive. I felt like he was cheating on me, though maybe not with actual intercourse or something like that, I knew and felt the energy was off between us. He kept denying it and blaming me for being crazy and for being jealous. A constant thing that showed up in my relationships. Things were getting so constricting and the physical connection less and less, the intuition more and more that I decided I had to find proof of it happening to convince myself I wasn't crazy. If I was crazy, I wanted to know. I went though his iPad. I found the proof. I confronted him with it after work and realized what he was doing while I was at work and he was home. He was addicted to porn. He was addicted to Instagram. Seeking outside validation and attention from others. He still denied it until I showed him what I found and he could deny it anymore. His reaction to me was that he really didn't know he was doing it.

Now some might think porn, and of course social media are ok. Anything in excess is not good, and porn ruins relationships. Any porn. I hold true to that, and I have so much experience being a woman, and also having had been addicted to watching it myself. I know. When you seek things outside of yourself, outside of your intimate relationship to seek fulfillment, it is only negative. I am not shaming anyone. Shame can turn anything, like eating a cupcake, into a negative energy. It's not about shame, it's about the energy of the connection and the relationships.

The other intuitive hits I got was him flirting with woman. Not just on social media apps, which he was doing, but also at work. I saw visions of it happening and confronted him with that as well. He admitted to it. Flirting is also cheating. It is a negative and also disrespectful to your relationship, and the partner you are with. When you become more and more sensitive, even the smallest things affect us just as much. We worked through it, I forgave him and we kept moving forward with the relationship. Also, I had to look at myself and see how I was also doing these things and not even realizing it either. Flirting was a hidden agenda of making myself feel wanted, and taking energy form the other person. We both course corrected and grew from the experience. We became more connected and our physical connection grew deeper. I started working through my addiction to sex with him. I realized we both had the same issues and we had to go real deep to release these addictions. I would become angry with him if he didn't have sex with me. It made me feel unloved and unattractive, something I was still seeking. Sex was love to me at the time. I felt unloved. We had to really work hard on this because it was so intimate, and ingrained and hard to find help with. I googled, he went to therapy. We restricted and talked and kept trying and trying. Eventually I felt the difference between making love with someone to having sex with someone. We both did.

As our connection got deeper, we were hit with something I didn't expect to happen. I had missed my period. it felt like something I had gone through before. A cycle repeating itself. My kids were with us for

Spring break, I was 6 weeks behind in cycle and then I started bleeding. I was thankful because it meant my period was here and I wasn't pregnant. About a few hours later I was doubled over in pain and excessive bleeding trying to decided if I needed to go toe Emergency room or not. I confided in him, my partner and he was not receptive or emotional enough to help me. I felt like I was having a miscarriage. He kept telling me that I was fine and that's not what's happening. I tried to convince myself that I was fine but I was in so much pain and I was bleeding so much, I bled through all my clothes, a tampon, pads and even the seat of my car when I tried to take my kids out and ignore the phase I was experiencing. I was having a miscarriage. I ended up laying in bed for 3 days, 2 of those days in complete pain, only getting up to bleed and have chunks of things leave me into the toilet. Something I never wish upon anyone. The worst part of it was that I felt alone. Even in a house with my boyfriend and my children. I hid it from them because I was embarrassed. It wasn't until I found a blog online that a woman wrote about her own experience did I truly believe the experience I was having too. It was word for word what I was feeling in my body. Unless you experience it, you really cannot say what it is. I had to confront him again about what I was feeling and needed him to validate it, instead of denying my truth. Again, it was difficult to go through. Again, we worked through. Again, we moved forward.

I had to trust myself. My body, and my mind.

Senior Year Portrait 1996

23

True Self

Suppressing my true self put me into a pattern of pain and suffering both physically and mentally. I stayed quiet and kept to myself. I was told that I needed to act like that because people would think I was different or weird and that was a bad thing. I was told not to tell people the things I saw, the future or how I knew things were going to happen before they did. How I talked and saw dead people. When I was 9 or 10 my dad came to visit me and it was the first time I had seen him in a long time. I remember him coming into my room to spend time together. I showed him things in my room, the toys I loved and then told him things about me. Instead of the warm embracing accepting thing to encourage me, he told me to shut down my true self. The world wasn't ready for people like me and so I was told to pretend that the things I saw didn't exist. Everything else around me also forced me to suppress who I was. My true self. I remember going into the bathroom and crying while he went to spend time with my sister. I know he was trying to protect me but that was him projecting his own stuff onto me. I know he tried his best and I forgive him for that.

As an adult I was a little more myself but still not fully owning it. The older I got, the more I started to hide and revert back to being a little girl because the more I tried to be myself, the less people seemed to like me. I wore a different hat around every person and it was exhausting. I catered my personality to what I thought they needed me to be.

That was a result of suppression combined with childhood trauma. It's a very depressing and unhealthy way to live on the inside.

Suppressing your true self is painful. It made me reject myself and wish that I was "normal." I wanted to be just like everyone else. No one is actually normal. Please remember that every single one of us wants to "fit in" and the truth is the people you want to fit in with are thinking the very exact same thing you are so what's the real problem? The real problem is society and our family and our friends and even ourselves when we live in a place of fear. "I'm afraid that my family won't love or support me anymore." Well what if they love you MORE? If they love you less then that's their problem and something you were born to change. We get put into families sometimes in order to help change the entire family dynamic, trust me it's a difficult one.

The truth is some of you may actually lose family members love and support but if you stay hidden then you are not only doing yourself a disservice, but also a disservice to those around you as well. More and more of us were born to make change, to force people to look at things differently. If we don't live as ourselves then we can't make people's points of view change. By hiding in the dark we are not raising our vibration and not helping to spark change around us, and eventually the world. You see, you are a very, very, very powerful soul that was meant to be different for a reason!

When I started to change and shed the layers of trauma it started to point me in the direction of loving myself. When I started to love myself more I naturally started to become a little brighter and more of my true self.

The more and more bodywork I did as a massage therapist, the more and more sensitive I became. I started knowing when and where people had cancer, or holding onto emotional baggage. When I did pregnancy massages I knew the sex of the baby before asking. I was 100 percent accurate. I even had one mother who didn't know but was curious at my thought and said she would come back to tell me if I was right. I had quit before she was able to but I have zero doubt that I was in fact right.

I ended up working as a massage therapist for less than a year at a spa. I not only was sensitive to the clients, but I became sensitive to the environment as well. My arms became tight and were starting to cause me an enormous amount of pain. No matter what I did physically the pain wouldn't leave me. I cut my schedule in half and the pain still wouldn't subside. I knew it wasn't what I was doing. It was the feelings, the gut feeling I had of suppressing what I was actually meant to do that was causing me pain. I wasn't in the right job and I was ignoring it. What better way than to show me. I work with my hands and you're going to make my hands hurt so much that I can barely move them? And I STILL didn't get it?! Of course it's ridiculous to me now looking back. But we can't see what we can't see.

By this time I had blamed it on my physical weaknesses. I told myself that I was weak and that message wasn't meant for weak people like me and I had to figure out some other way to make a living because I literally couldn't use my hands anymore. I was in so much pain that I couldn't open a jar. It hurt to do anything with my hands. The thought that I was too weak to massage was so ridiculous, especially because there were a few women who were the same size as me, if not even smaller, who were working triple the amount I was without any pain whatsoever! I was just not meant to stay there and I couldn't see it having just spent so much time, energy and money on getting to that place. I was heartbroken and so frustrated. I also knew there had to be something I was missing, and knew I had to keep following a path that had been laid out for me long before I was born into this life.

I found a workshop I thought would help me to get clients in another area I was interested in and possibly an alternative job setting.

It didn't exactly go the way I wanted it to. I thought I was following my life's purpose to Utah in order to help people with a certain process of healing trauma which was a type of age regression, talk therapy hypnotherapy type of thing.

I thought it was what I was supposed to do. I was wrong but I was also completely correct.

I knew I needed to go there in order to find attunement and connection. It was the reason why I was terrified to go and why I didn't want to go, at all. I am in a field of work where I need to have a connection and be attuned with people and yet I only want to be alone and not get involved with other people's lives. But if there's anything I have learned in my years it's that if I face the things that I fear or give me anxiety then it's when I find the most growth. I went to Utah to go work with a process I had never even heard of. I bought the book the day before I left on the airplane. It terrified me and I felt the nausea and anxiety building the closer I got there. My intuition got more and more clearer the closer I got. The first day we went over the process for a few hours and I had no idea what I was doing. I thought the whole week was learning the actual process but they actually expected you to already know it and spend the week just practicing it. I love being faced with these types of situations. It's terrifyingly eye opening. I had planned on reading the book on the airplane on the way there. Unfortunately, my anxiety got the best of me and I felt like I had to puke the entire way there and didn't get more than about 5 pages into it.

We were immediately thrown into the depths of unresolved trauma and triggers within each other. As I started to facilitate a practice client I kept getting in the way of myself. Tripping over all of my notes and scribbles that I had made in about 2 minutes by just skimming the book looking for the list of steps figuring I would just go with it. But the time came to put into practice what I didnt even learn yet. I stumbled and tripped myself up terribly. My group leader came over to help me with whispers and suggestions. I had to just listen to my intuition and I looked at her and said "He needs my presence only for grounding and he needs your confidence and words." She quickly took over the session and we went on a rollercoaster of having a part of himself being reborn through a long process of resolving unconscious trauma. I sat across from him, channeling and attuning to him to be present with him as he went on this rollercoaster. I felt everything he felt. My body experienced everything he had experienced as an infant in his mothers womb. I saw in my third eye being reborn through the birth canal. If anyone said that happened to them the day before I came there I would have said it was impossible. And there I sat having actually experienced it. After the group leader left us to calm down from that time traveling experience he looked over at me and said "I feel like I was reborn." Not telling him yet what I had experienced in my body and mind, I laughed really hard. I replied with "Yea, I know, I just felt and saw the whole thing." He then replied with "I was a c-section baby." I replied with laughter again and said "No wonder you had to be reborn through a birth canal." Then I explained to him everything I saw in my mind's eye and our experiences matched exactly.

That experience showed me how in tune I can be with someone else, a complete stranger from India, a different culture, and from a whole different part of the world. Exactly what the universe wanted to show me.

I worked with someone else and it was even stronger this time. By the third time I understood what was happening. Yet I also didn't know a damn thing about it. I felt possessed yet present. I was them but I was me. I just thought I was in total attunement. And I was attuned to a fault....according to the people that were putting on the workshop. They said they could not certify me or give me a certificate of completion because I was a channeler. I never even heard of the word "channeler" until I went there. Even more specific is that I am so into my subconscious and they literally want me to be more connected with the conscious instead. To me it sounded like they wanted me to be more human and less esoteric. That sure is confusing when you're at a spiritual retreat and learn that the person putting on the retreat is a channeler.

I went to my group leader to talk about the confusion and she worked with my channeled part of myself and she specifically asked who the channeled part was. It answered "Everything and nothing."

So there I sat, alone, having left the retreat early because even surrounded by 60+ "spiritual people" and I am still an outcast. I will say that I never have felt so understood, and so connected to such a large group of people before and for that I am still very thankful.

I found a connection. I found that part of me that I have tried so hard to ignore. I found everything and nothing. I say nothing because as I have come to realize at this point there is so much contradiction to everything. The everything and nothing statement did not come from me, it came to me. And it makes more and more sense to me everyday. Nothing is not nothing. You need the nothing in order to have something. The space between is just as important as the things in the space. For one cannot exist without the other.

There were 3 days left of the workshop and a group leader came up to me telling me I was not going to receive a certificate if I didn't start obeying the way the person putting on the retreat wanted me to be. I was totally shocked and then again not at all. Here was my moment. The moment where I needed to stand up and claim my true self. What would you have done? I later found out that people were paying attention to us and watching the whole thing unfold that I am about to share with you now.

While the group leader was talking my heart started racing and I started getting hot and sweaty. I felt my blood start to boil and at the same time I started to tremble and my face felt like it was going to start freaking out and release tears of rejection. But as she continued to talk I started a self dialogue within my head. I calmed myself down and told myself this is the moment. My intuition was telling me THIS is what you were here for. To claim yourself back. To take my power back. Stand up for what you believe to be true. Be your true, authentic self and stand up to the authority that is trying to keep you down. So that's exactly what I did.

When she finished talking I looked at her and explained that I understood where she (and they) were coming from but it goes against what is the right way, or in the best interest for the clients. The right way to treat people is by what the client needs, NOT by what you *think* they need. This is a bit tricky to understand and it will be left for another time and place. But if you do understand exactly what I mean then you know it's not about the ego, it's about the healing and what the soul needs in order to become whole. They let ego get in the way. I rejected the idea of lowering my standards to meet theirs for a piece of paper. My self worth was not going to be measured by that paper, even if it cost me a few thousand dollars to get there from a Go Fund Me account. I will fight for truth and justice over ego any day. The last 3 days of the retreat I was not allowed to participate but I showed up to it anyway because the food was all inclusive. I wasn't going to go run and hide. I was going to make the most out of what I paid for and find more good opportunities there despite them trying to hide me. The so called spiritual guru charging us thousands of dollars had many rules and zero interactions with us. Something I found suspicious. Even more suspicious, to me, was her way of dismissing her own triggers and refusing to do things with us because of them. How on earth are you going to teach people how to face their own trauma and triggers and then sit there making a joke how you're not facing your own? If you cant live your truth then you are living a lie.

I sat at the airport as I waited for a flight back east at midnight in Salt Lake City. I spent the day with a few others from the retreat and what started off as a great day ended in me crying. We went to the botanical gardens to find a nice place to sit and maybe do some work we had learned. We ended up not doing that at all. We talked about energy all day and the abilities we have and how it affects our lives. After a few hours there I decided they needed time to be alone. I went off to walk around and explore. I decided I would sit and try to channel the universe to see why I have the pain in my fingers. It didn't answer me. At all. Then my worst fear came true. The abilities I had had over those 10 days were all gone. So now what? What does that mean? I sat there and the shadow of self doubt slowly crept over me. I sat there and tried to analyze why I had this experience and then all of a sudden everything had stopped suddenly. I realized after contemplation that it was because I was trying too hard. I had expectations and wanted it so bad that it disappeared. Like the yoga pose you work at for years, then get it and it boosts your ego, only the next day it vanishes just as quickly. It's a lesson in ego and also in understanding that all things are in fact temporary.

I never even heard of channeling and then I became someone who did it. This is how my life apparently decided it wanted to unfold in this dimension. Over and over again I seem to have to go through experiences and then make sense out of them later on. While I think about it today I understand it more, but while it was happening over and over again as I searched for more and more answers and found nothing until after I experienced it, I got increasingly more and more impatient and frustrated. I sit here today in full understanding that the only way I could trust myself is by trusting my process and that process was solely by learning through my own experiences first, letting my ego selves experience and then let the brain decipher it, dissect it from every single angle, and then once I get it, be validated by truth elsewhere of that exact thing. Over and over and over again.

That weekend I came home to a packed full schedule of massage appointments at the spa. I woke up with the feeling and knowing that I would not be able to work there any longer. I ignored it anyway. I went to my tarot cards and asked for a sign. It proved my intuition and I ignored it anyway. As I walked to my car to go to work a neighbor, who I see often and usually just say hi back and forth, offered yet another sign to quit. He said "You better just turn right back around and go home." I laughed knowing it was the universe still trying to prove it to me. After all, I am still new to this and still am the biggest skeptic. (Always question everything! Even what I am writing!)

I went into work and my guides and intuition still told me I needed to quit. I clocked in and looked at the schedule as I asked my co-workers what had happened to the manager who suddenly got fired. I knew the answer before they responded. My guide told me she was fired because the new owners were not happy with the amount of money our location was making and found blame in her. They didn't tell her or any of the workers that of course. They blamed her for not communicating properly but that's not actually the truth. I asked my guide if I could please do the massages I was there to do and I got a *no*. I got that I could not work for a place that was so evil. Then I was showed the evil, and felt in my body in order to prove it to me. Money is not evil, but greed is. I got that I would always be taken care of and was shown my future. I'm still skeptical but I know now to listen. And trust. And have faith. I looked at my coworkers, wrote my name and phone number on the wall and told them *I quit*. I walked out with a full book, with nowhere to go, and no job to make money.

I knew I needed to take ownership of who I really am. I put it on social media and even updated my website to open up my possibilities for work. What I didn't know was that there was a storm brewing. When you open yourself up and are vulnerable to the world you might be surprised as to how people may react to you. I knew people I haven't talked to in years would probably just roll their eyes, and maybe even unfollow me and that doesn't mean anything to me. What I didn't think would happen was that it would affect my family in the way that it did. One family member in particular caused havoc. She told me I needed to see a therapist, asked me if I had a disease and told me I needed to be locked up. She then called my entire family to tell them this as well. She even called my father, who she hadn't spoken to in years, in order to just try to make people see what she saw. The sad thing was that it worked on a few of them and I ended up having to just block all of those family members on my social media accounts.

My friends and people I know have also been affected. They look at me and are scared of me. One yoga student I had said "I don't want you to know anything about me." I am sure many other people think the same things. I will say this: I don't want to know things about you either. This is why I need to be a strong person, have boundaries and have respect for this gift. I don't read people unless they ask. I don't get information and guidance unless I actively seek it. Sometimes though I do have spirits who have crossed over who will not leave me alone until I do something about it, and I do have guidance from my spirit that I don't ask for but it's for a greater purpose that sometimes I am not aware of.

The biggest issue, besides having to leave my job, leaving family and some friends behind was how it had affected my ability to be in an intimate relationship.

When someone looks at you from an outside perspective it is always difficult to hear. Especially when someone points out the things you need to work on.

I was in the middle of my own relationship and my true self as a psychic. Being a match to me means you are special (and maybe a little crazy). Being a match to a medium and a psychic is extremely difficult. We are very connected, all the time. We talk about energy and the universe, the stars and the sky and sometimes it makes sense and sometimes it really doesn't.

With every loss we encounter in life, it's for a bigger purpose that sometimes we may not be aware of, or even be ready for but just know that it's the universe's way of giving us an even bigger gift.

There's something that happens when you start living your purpose. It feels familiar yet strangely terrifying at the same time. It's hard to articulate into words but there is a feeling in the heart because it knows what your brain just can't rationalize yet. It knows who you really are, your brain is just a little behind in figuring it all out.

The other thing I wanted to say is that we cant please everyone. People like us want to make everyone else around us happy, most of us healers are people pleasers and that takes away from our energy, and away from the light of the creator. We have to be true to who we are if we ever want to live a happy and fulfilling life, one with purpose and laughter, love and joy. It can be difficult, it can be hurtful to have friends and family reject us, but it's worth it in the end. Eventually some of them come back around and will tell you straight to your face that you helped them, others you will never see again. Thats their journey and this is ours. We all have paths and they are all leading towards the light. Some just might take a lot longer than others. Thats doesn't make it any less spiritual or wrong. All is valid and right.

I started working for myself. I had a massage table to do massage out of my house and experimented with doing free psychic readings until I felt comfortable enough to start charging for it. I also started to do energy work, combining my psychic abilities with the Reiki that I learned in school. What resulted was a channeled protocol from Archangel Michael. I was guided to call it something with specific words, write it all down, make it a class to teach others and so I did. That is how Energy Channeling Healing was created. I trademarked it and made an outline and taught many people how to do it for themselves and others. I quit the spa with a giant leap of faith and put my trust in the universe, fully. I did 10 free psychic readings and my work spoke for itself. By word of mouth alone, I was booked for 3 months in advance.

24

The Ego Identity

Time to rebuild my identity, who I am and what I want out of this thing we call life. My life has been everything but linear and it remains that way to this day. My ego was once very small and something that only made me a human being and lifeless inside of a shell. Today my ego has gone through many transformations and many identities. Shifts and struggles in this current lifetime in this current dimension. I sit here today with an understanding of why I went through every single little thing that I have gone through in my life. Not only the good ones but also the bad and accepting all of them for what they are, things to make me grow and become who I was here to become me. Me, as in the pure vessel of light, to transform that light from above and throw me into everyone that needs it and when they need it, all at the perfect time. I was once a small child with low self-esteem, someone that hated herself and wanted nothing more than to die. Then I became a teenager that had nothing but a rebellious act pushing her forward. I wanted nothing more than to take everything down with me. I then became a wife and then a mother and part of a happy loving relationship. Next, I became someone that hid herself not only from herself but also hid from everything that is this universe. I thought that I needed to protect myself because I had not worked through the trauma that I had experienced in this lifetime and many others. I blamed other people for how I felt and it took me many years to realize that I needed to look inward instead of placing blame on others. My ego identified with being a victim and always being a victim. When you come from a place of always being a victim, you keep yourself in a certain state of existence that is keeping your soul from your soul's journey. Your soul and the energy that you possess wants to elevate, it wants to raise up and go into the light. It wants to be one with the light and one with all things. One with the universe.

While in the state of victimhood I had realized many things. It was in that state that I saw the more I identified with being a victim, the more I actually became a victim. My energy towards identifying with victimhood only escalated me becoming a victim. It was a vicious cycle that was hard to see for what it truly was. Being a victim is living in a state of suffering and is in the cycle of death and rebirth. It is something that happens over and over and over and over again until and only until you are able to recognize that you are in fact perpetuating the pain and suffering. We attract what we are thinking and feeling at all times. If you are in a vibrational frequency of pain and suffering, then you will attract more of that frequency. It's literally physics. It is only once you realize that you have the capacity to change it that you are then able to get out of the cycle of being addicted to the pain and suffering and the cycles of rebirth. Same is not only for victimhood but for everything else once you identify with something, anything, it keeps you in that state and it will keep you there until you stop identifying with it. This is why while growing up I always hated labels. I never wanted to be labeled anything because once you were labeled then that was it you were put inside of a box and you were stuck there, you were stuck in that box that someone else labeled you as. I never identified with that I never wanted to be labeled as a box and put a sticker on it and that was me. It just didn't feel right to me. So as I grew up I always changed as they saw fit. I listened to different types of music. I hung out with different types of crowds of people, I would go to raves, I went to hard-core shows, I saw punk rock bands, I saw you play at Veterans Stadium, I did a wide array of different things because that's what I was drawn to. People were trying to label me as a freak or a weirdo, or a punk or anything they could but I never took to any of those labels it just wasn't me I was just me. I hung out with the nerds, the people that were really smart and I hung out with the people that had no friends. I was nice to them in school because I valued what everyone had to offer me and usually it was a kind smile or a hello. It could be that simple, or it could be more complex like I could ask someone for help because they were smarter than me or knew better than me. I just really got along with everyone and so I never fit inside of any box that anyone tried to put me in or label me as. It was the same for everything else and perhaps that's why I never really had any big illnesses either. It's just not something that made sense to me ever. And I understand why now I see that once someone labels themselves then they are stuck there. It creates the energy of that thing that you label yourself as and that's it you kept yourself at that and that's all you'll ever be. Illnesses and disease are the worst. When you get a diagnosis for something, a doctor tells you that this is what you have and then you identify with that diagnosis and say I have this, that's what I am. And you are doing yourself a huge disservice by accepting that. Don't ever expect anything that anyone else has to say about you. End of story. You have the capacity to change and grow and heal yourself from the inside out. If there's anything that I have learned from living this life on earth it is that we have the capacity to change and heal ourselves as long as we want to change. And I want to stress that you have to want to actually change. Because there are many many people that say they want to change but they never put forth the effort to actually change. They only convince themselves that by saying they want to change that it will make themselves better. That is a false sense of security because you don't actually want to change unless you do something about it. You have to take action behind the things that you were saying behind the words behind what you ultimately are striving to be and that is something better than you are today or yesterday. To always strive to be a better version of yourself and know that there is a way that you can heal and that you don't need someone else to give you permission to be a better version of yourself. You have the capacity and the tools are at your disposal within the world around you. Everyone and everything is trying to show you the way to a better self into a better life. You only have to be open and allow these messages to come to you.

Your ego is surrounding you as you walk through the day. It is the voice inside of your head and it is being reflected back to you by every person that you interact with. You have the capacity to change that for yourself. You have the authority over yourself. You are the only one that is responsible for your life. Take that responsibility into your own hands and make it the life that you have always dreamed of having. Start now, start today, and do something about it.

From here moving forward my ego is who I want to be. It is still a mother and it is a lover of all things, including all of the people that have hurt me the most. I love them all. I walk through my life now devoted to myself and to my mission of trying to change the world one person at a time. My hope with this book is that at least one person would have the understanding that they are not alone in any of this. And if that one person can feel like someone else understands where they are at then I would have a feeling of accomplishment. Because the whole reason I said all to write a story about my life is to help the version of me that was and felt completely utterly helpless and alone in solitude. I was thankful that I was able to go through these things so that I can be here today and help those that need help the most with my experiences in my words. I walk now with my head held high whether it's doing the laundry or if it's connecting with a friend who is reaching out for words of advice. My heart guides my way as I continue to learn and grow for my own soul journey and continue my quest of helping others.

My identity is anything that I want it to be and I'm only limited by my own imagination. I can literally be anyone I want to and I can change it at a moment's notice. It takes time and effort and work to do so but it is not something that is out of my reach. I have done it over and over again. I had one job and I quit for another job. It's the same as that, only it's just slightly different. You can change jobs if you don't feel like your current job fits you anymore. There are times when you outgrow your jobs, your relationships with friends and family and significant others.

When you change and grow if the people or jobs or surroundings are not also changing and growing with you then something drastic has to happen. But let's hope for the future that as we change and grow and evolve so well , more and more people and things surrounding us and so it will get easier as time goes by. Time period is in time a funny thing also another thing that we have made up a limiting belief that time is only what you make of it. Time is so much grander than a place. It's not just one thing, it is so much more and I cannot wait to meet you where I am now and where I will be, in what is called the future.

25

Rebirth

One significant change has occurred within your life: it is time to have a rebirth. When you hear the word rebirth it can mean so much more than just re-incarnation. In fact, I have had many numerous re-births within the same lifetime. This is often what people call awakening or some people call themselves born again. It is a similar concept but through my connection with channeling and the universe I have come to realize that the significance of being *born again* is so much deeper than anything I've ever thought about before. There are many clients that I have had that needed to have a rebirth to heal, solely because their actual physical birth into this life was so traumatic and in fact, there are many of them walking around with that same trauma attached to them from the moment they were born and brought into this human experience. It reminds me of the experience I had in Utah with that other student where I had literally helped him be born again through a delivery without having known previously that he was a C-section. The change that that created for him was evident as I watched him throughout the rest of the week. He came out of his shell. He started to feel ok about talking and initiating conversations. A rebirth is something that is so spiritual that you would not have any idea of just how important it was until you actually have gone through it. The first time I had my own rebirth I had to physically do it by burrowing myself under blankets and imagining that I was in the womb and using my own power and will to descend down the canal and breathing my new life into my lungs as I came out with my head first. Falling onto the floor off of my massage table and then acting infant like all over again for a brief moment until I was able to stand up on my own 2 feet. it may sound intense because it really was. It was so very visceral.

A rebirth for me now is generally a long soak in the bathtub with some nice essential oil's candles lit, maybe some music and just time with myself in the water. A cleansing that removes any residual energy out of my field and off of my physical body. A rebirth can be as simple as that or as even more intricate as driving two hours to dip yourself into the ocean into the salt water and having the waves rush over your body. I feel a very large rebirth coming very shortly, one that includes a trip somewhere tropical. One that I will not be alone with though the one person or a few that will be standing by me still remain faceless and nameless. I know it's coming. I can feel it within me. I know that when I go there I will feel complete. A cycle completing itself starting all over again from the very beginning of where I came from, whatever lifetime that is referring to I still am unaware of. It could be one from the past or from the future as we call it but what I do know is that something you just came for me and that when the wave of ocean water rushes over me I will know who I am inside and out and without a shadow of a doubt whatsoever. There will be no self-doubt left in me because I will know the answer and the steps I need to take in order to move forward into stepping into my soul's purpose once and for all.

26

The Ending Is Only The Beginning of The Next

There is no room for hatred, pity or for excuses in my life anymore. And once I change, the people around me change. The ones that end up staying in my life are the ones that tend to reflect the things I put out. I have been putting out so much love for everyone, that it is all coming back to me.

You are perfectly imperfect, exactly as you are, in every single moment. Society and people all around us judge us and so we end up living lives to try and not be judged yet it only makes us judge ourselves and others more and no one ends up happy. We can't live up to the expectations of others, or the false versions of ourselves and so we must learn to overcome these judgements and expectations of others and ourselves. We must change the narratives in our lives so that we can live in peace and harmony with ourselves, our bodies and our souls. It's the only way to raise our vibrations and to live a life of fulfillment. Follow your own heart and be the person you know you are inside. Don't be afraid to be yourself and to speak your truth.....no matter how many times you feel the need to. Do it often, just do it.

Life is full of battles, and it's not about winning or losing them. Life is about the lessons you learn along the way and how you react when things show up that are unpleasant. It's about being able to grow from them and never becoming a victim. You have a choice of how great your life will be. You have the power to change things. You have the power to forgive and to love yourself and everyone else with unconditional love. That is what life is about. Love.

Love is perfectly imperfect, never be afraid to say it out loud.
Life is perfectly imperfect, don't be afraid to live it.
You are perfectly imperfect, don't be afraid to be you.
~Jenifer

The Body Keeps the Score by Bessel van der Kolk

It Didn't Start with You: How inherited Family Trauma Shapes Who We Are and How To End The Cycle by Mark Wolynn

The Yamas and Niyamas: Exploring Yogas Ethical Practices by Deborah Adele

Ashtanga yoga: there are studios all around globe, look in your area or find one online. Videos are good, but it truly is meant to be guided step by step with a teacher.

Other therapies: There are many paths to healing and it is up to you to find them, and search them out. If you want to be pointed in the right direction for you, look at the people around you. See who comes into your reality. Do you know 3 massage therapists? Get a massage or learn more about it. Did you just meet someone who is into Tai Chi or Martial Arts? These people and things come into our lives for a reason. Trust it, follow the breadcrumbs. It may not make sense at the time, but TRUST me, it will later when you look backwards. It always does.

Jenifer has been practicing Ashtanga yoga since 2013, and has studied numerous modalities and healing techniques ranging from the physical to the very subtle. She is the creator of Energy Channeling Healing (EnergyChannelingHealing.com) and owns and operates PremaMateria.com. She works as a yoga instructor, energy healer, metaphysical practitioner and helps others to connect to their own psychic powers through mentorships and teaches students of Energy Channeling Healing how to heal themselves through energy. She has dedicated her life to showing others that there is a reason for everything and that there is no such thing as a coincidence.

2019 Philadelphia
self portrait

CPSIA information can be obtained
at www.ICGtesting.com
Printed in the USA
FSHW022116030122
87104FS

9 781087 997117